Beginning
Ethereum & Solidity
with React

Greg Lim

Table of Contents

PREFACE

About this book

In this book, we take you on a fun, hands-on and pragmatic journey to learning decentralized application (DApp) development on the Ethereum blockchain using the Solidity programming language. You'll start building your first Ethereum smart contract within minutes. Every section is written in a bite-sized manner and straight to the point as I don't want to waste your time (and most certainly mine) on the content you don't need. In the end, you will have what it takes to develop a real-life decentralized eBay Clone app.

In the first chapter, we see how Ethereum works and why do we care about it. In the second chapter, we will create our first working smart contract with Ethereum where we learn how to interact with Ethereum as developers.

We will then move on to chapters three and four where we will learn about compiling, deployment and testing of Ethereum apps. All these will prepare us for development of our decentralized eBay clone smart contract and the React user front end in chapter five and six.

The goal of this book is to teach you how to build decentralized apps with Ethereum. We won't be talking a lot about trading cryptocurrencies, how to invest in Ethereum or how to trade Ethereum (ether) coins. We will have a good overview of Ethereum and cryptocurrencies but we will not be going into super in-depth academic discussion of them as our focus in this book is to have the practical knowledge of how to work with and build products with Ethereum.

Requirements

No need to know anything about blockchain. But you should have basic software development experience whether web, mobile or backend.

Getting Book Updates

To receive updated versions of the book, subscribe to our mailing list by sending a mail to support@i-ducate.com. I try to update my books to use the latest version of software, libraries and will update the codes/content in this book. So do subscribe to my list to receive updated copies!

Contact and Code Examples

The source codes used in this book can be found in my GitHub repository at https://github.com/greglim81 (search for 'solidity' under 'Repositories')

Send any comments or questions concerning this book to support@i-ducate.com.

CHAPTER 1: INTRODUCTION TO ETHEREUM

A brief history of what led to Ethereum

Bitcoin was released in January 2009, and since then, it has been used to transfer money in a peer to peer blockchain network. We will talk about blockchain in detail through this book but a brief description of the Bitcoin blockchain is that it stores monetary transactions between different people. These transactions are independently verified by others and held on a distributed ledger which every node in the network owns a copy of.

There is no central or world bank entity that controls Bitcoin; it is a decentralized digital currency. And because there is no need for a central authority or middle man, you could pay another directly and thus save on payment transaction fees. The Bitcoin network continues to grow today.

But the only purpose of Bitcoin was to enable financial transactions, to send money from person A to person B. People soon realized that they could use Bitcoin innovations not just for transfer of currency, but to support complex apps providing other types of exchanges like buying and selling of products/services (e.g. eBay), insurance, gambling, crowd funding, voting, ownership and other many kinds of applications. Ethereum is one of the most prominent example of leveraging on the Bitcoin blockchain innovation.

Ethereum is an open programmable blockchain platform supported by a decentralized network of computers. It is used to transfer money between different parties (through its internal currency called *ether*) and lets anyone to to create and use decentralized applications (DApps) that run on blockchain technology. DApps are formed by one or more smart contracts. An Ethereum smart contract is a program that runs on Ethereum. These smart contracts allows users of Ethereum to create their own operations of any complexity they wish – therefore providing a platform for different types of decentralized blockchain applications including but not limited to cryptocurrencies.

The Case for De-Centralized Applications

You might ask of course, but aren't there already existing technologies that we can use to implement applications for buying/selling of products/services? Why specifically use Ethereum? Now almost all of the Internet based applications we have been using for a pretty long time are centralized. That is, servers of the application are owned by a particular company or person. However, there are some issues with centralized apps. They possibly have a single point of failure, if the company's server goes down, the app goes down (you can resolve that by having multiple servers in a distributed architecture). But more importantly, centralized apps are inevitable less transparent and companies/persons can possibly hold control over user data for example, censorship, selling your data to other companies and so on. A famous case that happened recently at this book's time of writing was the Facebook–Cambridge Analytica data scandal that involved the collection of more than 87 million Facebook users data possibly for political reasons, i.e. to influence voter opinion.

These concerns lead to the building of decentralized applications (DApp) which leverages on Bitcoin innovations. A DApp is also an application like many Internat based apps but the difference is that it runs on a decentralized peer to peer network with its source code being open sourced. Being distributed, DApps don't have a single point of failure. There is also no central authority who has complete control over the DApp, thus it gains users trust.

Smart Contracts – At the Core of Ethereum

The most important part that provides such functionality for Ethereum apps is the smart contract and that is where Ethereum differs mainly from Bitcoin in that Ethereum adds the functionality of the smart contract. The smart contract is a piece of code that lives in the blockchain. You can think of it as digital money that has logic associated with it without human intervention (thus making it trustworthy). Smart contracts generally transfer value from one account to another only if certain conditions are met. A real life use case of a smart contract in insurance could automatically pay out to the insured entity based on a data feed showing that a payable event had occurred. Or for a football game betting contract, payout would happen automatically based on the data feed of actual live football matches results. Contracts are at the absolute core of what Ethereum is. We will spend majority of this book to learn the behavior of these contracts.

In this book, we will learn the steps that will lead us up to developing a full decentralized eBay clone Ethereum application where users can post products for sale, and others to buy them (fig. 1.1 and 1.2).

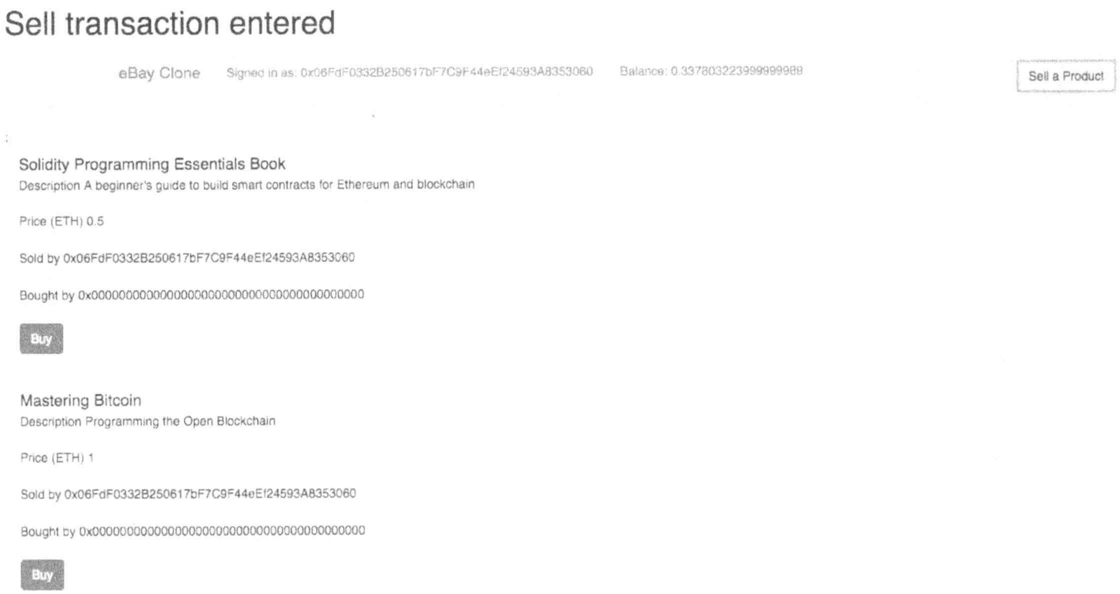

Sell transaction entered

figure 1.1

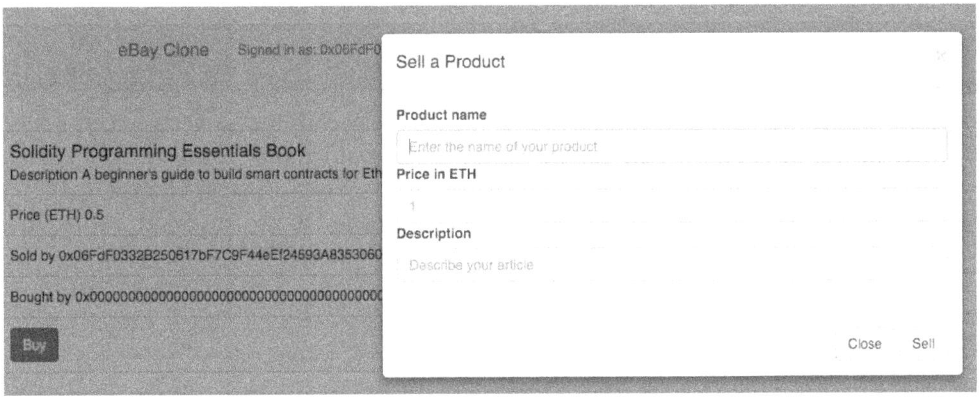

figure 1.2

In the process of developing our eBay clone, we will learn how to write a smart contract using the Solidity programming language, how to test and deploy the smart contract to test and main networks, and how to write a React Javascript front end that connects to our deployed smart contract so that users can interact with it as they do with normal websites. All of this will form our fully functional DApp using Ethereum.

Ethereum makes it easy for us to write DApps with smart contracts because we don't have to worry about how to implement the underlying blockchain technology, consensus protocol, proof of work algorithm and other things (don't worry if you don't understand some of the jargon used here, we will get to them in this book).

Other than smart contracts, every DApp also needs a client for users to use the DApp. That is the client should connect to a node in the network. In this book, we will create a client using React JavaScript which allows easy access and usage of our DApp.

Ethereum Networks

There is one main Ethereum network which is where ether coins are worth real money and production apps are deployed. There are many other test networks like the Ropsten, Kovan and Rinkeby test networks which are used for testing of smart contracts and transactions. You can even create your own private Ethereum network and open it to other people.

An Ethereum network is formed by one or more nodes. Each node is a machine (it could be a desktop, laptop or just any private computer) running an Ethereum client. Anyone can run a node by installing and running the Ethereum client software. Each node in the network has a full and separate copy of the blockchain. For now, you can think of the blockchain as a database that stores the records of every transaction that has ever taken place.

Interfacing with Ethereum Networks

You can connect to the Ethereum network as a normal user or as an Ethereum DApp developer. Normal users who do not develop smart contract code and whose main purpose is to send/receive money connect to Ethereum using a Chrome extension called MetaMask. There are other methods of connecting to the Ethereum network like the Mist browser. But as this point of writing, Mist is still in early beta and some functionality is still in development. MetaMask is more mature and in general easier to use. In this book, we will mainly be using web3.js and MetaMask to connect to the Ethereum network.

Ethereum DApp developers (I suppose that you are one since you are reading this book!) create apps that talk to the Ethereum network through a library called web3.js. web3.js acts like a portal to the network which allows us to send money, store data and deploy contracts. web3.js is hosted at https://github.com/ethereum/web3.js/ and you can find its documentation at https://github.com/ethereum/wiki/wiki/JavaScript-API.

MetaMask Setup

Whether you are a user or an aspiring Ethereum developer, we will now install MetaMask to create our Ethereum accounts.

We will first walk through the installation process of Metamask. In Chrome, open a new tab and navigate to the Chrome Web Store (https://chrome.google.com/webstore/).

Search for 'MetaMask' (fig. 1.3) and click 'ADD TO CHROME' to install.

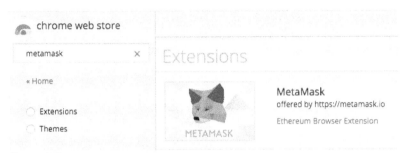

figure 1.3

Once MetaMask is installed, a new MetaMask icon will be shown to the right of the URL bar. Click on it and the UI will appear. Proceed with the steps as instructed and you will be prompted to enter a new password (fig. 1.4).

figure 1.4

Enter your new password to create a new Ethereum account. The account will allow you to send, receive ethers and also deploy smart contracts that we create.

figure 1.5

After entering your password and creating your account, you will be told that a vault has been created and you have twelve words which are the only way to restore your MetaMask account (fig. 1.5). As instructed, save the twelve words somewhere safe and secret. We will be using and explaining the usage of the twelve words in detail later in chapter four.

On the top left, you will see 'Main Network' (fig. 1.6). This means that you are connected to the main network which is the public production network where Ether coins have real value and real apps are deployed and used by users. You can select other test networks like Ropsten, Kovan and Rinkeby from the dropdown. You can also choose 'Localhost 8545' to host a local test Ethereum network on your machine. 'Custom RPC' allows you to connect to a remote Ethereum network at a remote address.

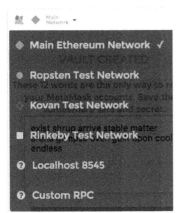

figure 1.6

Ethereum Account

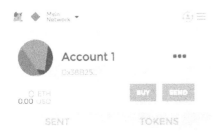

figure 1.7

Under your account name, you will see a weird string of characters e.g. '0x38B25…' (fig. 1.7). This weird string of characters is actually a hexadecimal value that represents your Ethereum account address similar to an email address or username. It's a unique identifier that tells people who you are. Your account will also come with a public and private key. The public and private are used together to authorize the sending of funds from your account to someone else's account. One will need the private key of an account to access the funds assigned to that particular account. Without it, you cannot access the account's funds. You can access your private key by clicking on 'Export Private Key'. But you should never share your private key with others as whoever gets your private key can easily get access to your account.

An Ethereum Transaction

Whenever we transfer ether from an account to another account or to a contract, invoke methods of a contract, or deploy a new contract, we are actually creating an Ethereum transaction. An Ethereum transaction is a signed data package with a couple of properties. We present the main ones below:

to: the address ether coins is sent to

value: amount of ether to be sent

startGas/gasLimit: maximum number of computational steps the transaction execution is allowed to take

gasPrice: the cost the sender of the transaction is willing to pay for each computational step

nonce: a number that tells you the number of transactions sent from a given address.

The below shows the information of an actual transaction extracted from etherscan.io (fig. 1.8):

Transaction Information

TxHash:	0xc4f08b5e7e02a0376091df59849f024182a51bd8f37
TxReceipt Status:	Success
Block Height:	5649307 (1 block confirmation)
TimeStamp:	30 secs ago (May-21-2018 01:54:20 AM +UTC)
From:	0x16ff98a65e60c9893592b0e294b7409c60c902cc
To:	0x295a66b8bef63661178f271c2b30630f3a8ea100
Value:	0.005783752 Ether ($4.10)
Gas Limit:	21000
Gas Used By Txn:	21000
Gas Price:	0.000000006 Ether (6 Gwei)
Actual Tx Cost/Fee:	0.000126 Ether ($0.09)
Nonce & {Position}:	13	{221}

Figure 1.8

What Goes On Behind a Transaction?

Ethereum has to be robust and secure enough to handle transations of billions/trillions of dollars between people everyday. Representing transactions of such huge value between different parties in a secure manner is obviously very complex.

A transaction is first sent to one interfacing node and that node will communicate with the rest of the network. At any moment, there might be multiple transactions. These multiple transactions are assembled as a list of transactions referred to as a block.

For example, in the below figure 1.9, we have block 5649322 which contains 107 transactions and 9 contract internal transactions.

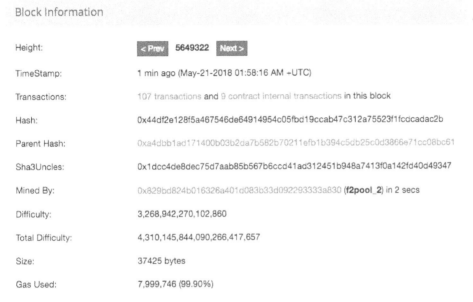

Figure 1.9

The 107 transctions contained in block 5649322 are shown in figure 1.10.

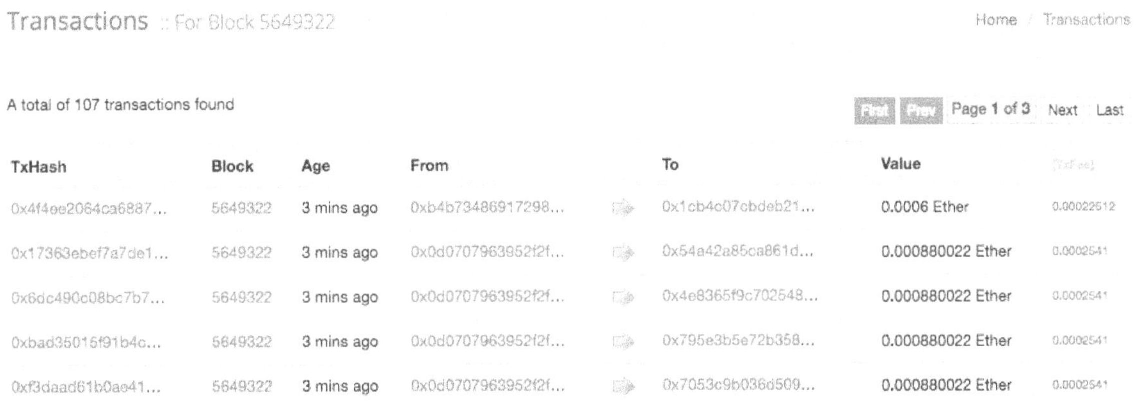

Figure 1.10

For e.g.:

Transfer 0.0006 ether from 0xb4b734... to 0x1cd4c0...
Transfer 9.999880022 ether from 0x0d0707... to 0x54a42a...
and so on.

Mining a Block and Block Time

To mine a block, first of all a miner collects the new unmined transactions broadcasted to it. The miner creates a block with the transactions and creates a hash with the data in the transactions and a nonce. i.e. *data + nonce = hash*

The computation challenge is to create a hash when converted to a base 10 number to be less than some target value. Such a hash is a valid hash or what Ethereum terms as a 'proof of work'. Since the data in the transactions are fixed and cannot be altered, the only way to come up with a valid hash is to trial and error different nonce values till *data + nonce = hash* converted to base 10 number is less than or equal to the target value, thereby making the block valid.

The amount of iterations that has to be taken to find the hash less than the target value takes some amount of time. The computer has to execute many hashes (easily hundreds of thousands of different hashes) to find the one whose base 10 is less than the target value. And this is even harder when the target value is lowered. We refer to the time taken to find a hash base 10 number less than target value as 'Block Time'. And once a node finds the solution, it then distributes that solution to other nodes.

The Ethereum network has a target block time of 10-20 seconds. It is important to keep the block time at a constant because users will want to know to how much time it should take for a transaction to be completed. Thus, the network looks at the time it took to calculate the previous block and if it seems that it took too long to generate a valid hash, it will raise the target value (thereby lowering the difficulty) so that a miner can find the solution more quickly.

The whole point of having valid hashes is to make block creation computationally hard, there by preventing attackers from remaking the entire blockchain in their favor. We will explain more of this in the section below 'Security of a Blockchain'.

The Blockchain Datastructure

Blocks 'chain' together to form a blockchain. The blockchain is thus a data structure (or a 'glorified' linked-list) that chain several blocks together in a serialized manner by having each block containing the hash of the previous block in the *prev* property (see example below).

Block 5 | nonce : 0x6893... | data: ... | prev: 0xc35f... | hash: 0x52c9...

Block 4 | nonce : 0x20f5... | data: ... | prev: 0x2dbd... | hash: 0xc35f...
Block 3 | nonce : 0x0162... | data: ... | prev: 0xa6ec... | hash: 0x2dbd...
Block 2 | nonce : 0x1843... | data: ... | prev: 0xdc6d... | hash: 0xa6ec...
Block 1 | nonce : 0x995f... | data: ... | prev: 0x2129... | hash: 0xdc6d...
Block 0 | nonce : 0x0000... | data: ... | prev: 0x0000... | hash: 0xd4e5...

*For block #1, *prev* is 0000 since there are no previous blocks before it. It is also known as the genesis block. You can infact see the Ethereum genesis block at https://etherscan.io/block/0.

Security of a Block Chain

Now if someone tampers with the data for a previous block, it would change its hash, and the *prev* of the next block will not match it thus breaking the block and subsequent blocks. The tamperer will have to go on and attempt to remine each subsequent block.

And if a tamper occurs further back in the chain, more subsequent blocks have to be remined. It is therefore harder and harder to make changes as we go back in time to previous blocks. And that's how a blockchain resists change to existing data and therefore automates auditing making the application transparent and secure. It prevents DApps from fraud and corruption.

Also, in a distributed blockchain, each node has a copy of the blockchain. And if data changes only in one node, we can tell that something is wrong with that node's blockchain because even though the blockchain might be valid, it's hash differs from other nodes. And to detect that, we don't have to look at all the hashes for all the blocks. We can just look at the hash of the latest block in the chain since the different hash values gets propagated up to the latest block chain.

Summary

In this chapter, we covered a brief history of the Bitcoin innovations in particular the blockchain that led to Ethereum. The fact that the Ethereum blockchain is programmable gave rise to the building of decentralized applications on it. Smart contracts being the core of Ethereum will be the focus of the rest of the chapters. In the next chapter, we begin developing a simple smart contract with Solidity.

CHAPTER 2: INTRODUCTION TO SMART CONTRACTS

Smart contracts are what we use to build interesting applications on the Ethereum blockchain. Remember that a smart contract is an Ethereum account controlled by code deployed on the blockchain that has logic to transfer value from one account to another only if certain conditions are met. This code is developed by developers like you and me. The code instructs the smart contract how to behave. Accounts controlled by contract code is also known as a contract account. In contrast, accounts owned by humans are known as external accounts.

Properties contained in a smart contract:
balance - amount of ether controlled by this account
storage - data storage for related data for this contract. This data is related to whatever application we are building. e.g. numbers, strings, arrays, any type of data relevant to the app.
code - raw machine code for this contract. The code that we write in our code editors are going to be compiled down to this raw machine code and it's stored inside the contract.

The Solidity Programming Language

We write smart contracts in a programming language known as Solidity. There are other languages which you can write smart contracts in like LLL and Serpent, but Solidity is the most popular of the languages. It has many features inside the language to make the execution of these contracts much easier. We write smart contracts in Solidity source files using the *.sol* extension.

After writing our Solidity code, we then feed it into a Solidity compiler which gives two outputs, byte code and the Application Binary Interface or ABI. The byte code is the actual code that is deployed and executed on the Ethereum network. The ABI is important for writing user front ends that can interact with our deployed smart contracts. For example in this book, we will write JavaScript code that serves to be the front end user interface of our app. The ABI provides an interface for our JavaScript code to interact with our deployed smart contract byte code.

The ABI is something that is legible so we can read it to give us a good idea of how we can interact with our contract. The ABI allow us to get a good idea of what functions and data we can call and interact inside of the deployed smart contract. We will show in the next chapter an example of a smart contract ABI.

Deployment of a Smart Contract

After we have coded our contract, we can deploy it to a test network like Rinkeby or the actual main network. When we deploy this contract code, an instance of the contract is created on the network. Each contract instance will have it's own contract address. We can take one contract file which contains the contract source code and deploy it multiple times (thus multiple instances) to an Ethereum network. This is very similar to the relationship between a class and an instance in programming. The contract source code serves as a class. Like a class, a contract contains variables, functions, structs and so on. It defines the behaviour of a contract where we then create multiple instances of that contract by deploying them to a specific network.

Using Remix to Write our First Smart Contract

We are going to start writing our first Solidity smart contract. We will use an online code editor called Remix. Remix is made specifically for creating and testing Solidity contracts. We can use any code editor of course but Remix has a lot of built in tools to code, compile, run, test and debug our code. We will later write our code in an editor but for now, we will grasp smart contract concepts better by using Remix.

To begin, go to remix.ethereum.org. There, you will immediately see a bunch of code in the browser code editor (fig. 2.1).

Figure 2.1

The default code can be overwhelming so we will start with a simpler code. By the end of this book, you will be able to understand the default code. So in Remix editor, select all the code and delete it. We will start with a very simple contract from scratch.

Enter the following codes into the Remix editor (fig. 2.2):

Figure 2.2

```
pragma Solidity ^0.4.23;

contract Greetings{
  string public message;

  constructor(string initialMessage) public {
    message = initialMessage;
  }

  function setMessage(string newMessage) public {
    message = newMessage;
  }
}
```

Code Explanation

Before we compile and run the code, let's have a walk through and explanation of the code.

```
pragma Solidity ^0.4.23;
```

We specify the version of Solidity that our code is written with the *pragma* directive. As time of writing, the latest stable version is 0.4.23.

```
contract Greetings{
```

With the keyword *contract*, we define a new contract 'Greetings' that will have some number of methods and variables. Remember that *contract* here is similar to *class*! We deploy a contract to the Ethereum network and the deployed version is an instance of the contract (you can deploy multiple instances of a contract and each instance is identified by its unique address).

21

```
string public message;
```

We declare a storage instance variable *message* of type *string* that exist in the life of a contract instance. With the *public* keyword, this variable is made accessible to anyone in the world. Whatever value we assign to *message* will be stored for eternity in the block chain. That is, we can always pull our contract back up from the block chain and look at the value of the variable. Such variables are also known as state variables. This is in contrast to local variables (e.g. variables declared within a function) which are created temporary when a contract is executed and thrown away at the very end.

```
constructor(string initialMessage) public {
  message = initialMessage;
}
```

With the *constructor* keyword, we define our constructor function which is automatically called when a contract is first created and deployed to the blockchain. Our constructor function takes in an argument *initialMessage* of string type which is then assigned to the contract's *message* variable. Constructors typically are used to initialize state variables. We will see later in Remix how to instantiate contracts and call a constructor function (and other functions) with arguments.

```
function setMessage(string newMessage) public {
  message = newMessage;
}
```

We define a *setMessage* function which we can call on the contract after it has been deployed on the blockchain.

Now, we have a *setMessage* function, why don't we have a *getMessage* function? We can! The below would serve as a *getMessage* function.

```
function getMessage() public view returns (string){
  return message; // return only use in function with 'view'
}
```

Note that in *getMessage()*, the method header has the *view* keyword which indicates to the Solidity compiler that this function does not attempt to change any data in the contract. It only 'views' the *message* data and doesn't modify it. We also have the keyword *returns (string)* in the method header which indicate that this method returns a value of string type.

Now, the reason why I have not added a *getMessage()* function into the code is that by default, any variable declared as *public* will have a getter function automatically generated. That is, *message* will have a getter function automatically generated, and that is why I have not included it in the code. We will see this concretely in the next few sections as we run and test our contract in Remix.

22

Also, note that functions that attempt to change value in a contract like *setMessage* cannot be marked as *view* and neither can they contain a *return* statement. We will cover more function types as we go along.

Compiling with Remix

At this point in time, when you click on 'Start to Compile', you should see a green box labeled 'Greetings' at the side which indicates successful compilation (fig. 2.3). Remix has a Solidity compiler which compiles our Solidity code into byte code and deploys an instance of our Greetings contract to an in-browser fake Ethereum network. This is useful for testing purposes as we will see in the next section.

Figure 2.3

If there are any compilation errors, they will appear in red (fig. 2.4).

Figure 2.4

Testing with Remix

We will now use Remix to test our contract. Behind the scenes, Remix is not just a code editor, it also hosts a mini fake Ethereum network that we can use to simulate deploying and interacting with our contract which makes Remix a very useful tool. Remix also provides a console on the bottom that describes what is happening in our in-browser network.

Now you can choose to click on the "auto-compile" checkbox to avoid having to manually click 'Start to Compile' each time you do a code change.

To start running your contract, click on the 'Run' tab where you will see a couple of settings (fig. 2.5):

Figure 2.5

Environment: has the following options, JavaScript VM, Injected Web3, Web3 Provider. For now, choose JavaScript VM which refers to the in-browser virtual Ethereum network.

Account: When we choose JavaScript VM, a handful of different test accounts is created. Each is assigned 100 ether which makes testing easier for us. i.e. we can simulate transfer of ether between accounts. Remember that these accounts exist only in our browser right now.

Gas Limit: maximum number of computational steps the transaction execution is allowed to take

Value: You specify how much ether you want to send along in a transaction.

In the next panel, you have a dropdown which currently shows our 'Greetings' contract.Now if we have multiple compiled contracts, the dropdown will contain the list of contracts we can deploy to our local browser based test network.

Beneath that, you will see an input field with "string initialMessage" and a 'Create' button to the right. This is actually the constructor function that we have in our Solidity code which is automatically called when we deploy our contract. When we enter in some string and click 'Create', an instance of our Greetings contract is automatically created and the construction function is called. Whatever we type in the input box is assigned to *initialMessage* variable in our contract.

Now, type "Hello World!" and make sure that you enclose them in double quotes. Click 'Create'. ***

You should see the console logging "creation of Greetings pending..." and some other transaction details. You will get to understand them throughout the course of this book. For now, we will move on to testing our contract.

```
creation of Greetings pending...
[vm] from:0xca3...a733c, to:Greetings.(constructor), value:0 wei,      Details   Debug
data:0x608...00000, 0 logs, hash:0x8fb...749c7
>
```

Upon creation of the contract, you will see a new entry representing our instance of the Greetings contract that we have just deployed to our local test fake network.

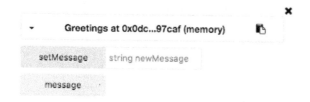

All the different functions of our instance are listed as buttons. i.e. *message*, *setMessage*. When we click any of them, it invokes the corresponding function in our contract. Buttons in blue are 'view' or 'constant' functions that can be called and some data is returned to us. This is how we can interact with our contract in Remix. Notice that a getter function for *message* our public variable is automatically generated. Now you see why we do not need a *getMessage()* function?

The *setMessage* function modifies some content of the contract and has an input just like the constructor which tells us what type of input it is expecting if we want to call it. i.e. *string*.

If we click on *message*, we see in the console 'call to Greetings.message' followed by
"0": "string: Hello World"
This means that data of *string* type with actual value 'Hello World' is the first return value from the function. In our case, the function returns only one value.
If the function returned multiple values, we would see
"0": "..."
"1": "..."

```
call to Greetings.message

[call] from:0xca35b7d915458ef540ade6068dfe2f44e8fa733c, to:Greet    Details    Debug
ings.message(), data:e21f3...f37ce, return:
{
        "0": "string: Hello World"
}
```

Try it out

Now try calling *setMessage* with a different string and then call *message*. Do you see the console log with the updated value?

Although our contract doesn't do anything much right now, it illustrates how anyone on the network can call *message* and *setMessage* on our deployed Greetings contract.

Re-deploying our Contract

Note that if we make a code change, we have to compile and re-deploy the contract in Remix. Else, you will still be be running the instance of the previous code. Also, to delete a previous instance of the contract, click on the 'X' on the top right of the contract instance panel.

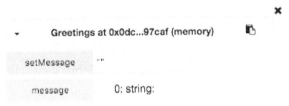

After you have compiled your modified code, proceed on to click 'Create' with the necessary construction parameters to deploy a new instance of the contract.

Behind the Scenes of Deployment

What happens when we deploy our contract by clicking on the 'Create' button? Creating a contract is also considered as submitting a transaction to store the deployed contract with the value of *message* in the blockchain. The transaction properties for contract creation is that the person creating the contract is the 'sender'. The 'To' field is left blank. The 'data' property holds the compiled byte code of the contract. Do note that the byte code is available for everyone else in the world to read just as anything deployed onto the blockchain. So don't put any secret business logic because it's exposed to the world.

A contract can also have an initial ether value assigned by specifying the 'value' property. So we can deploy a contract with an initial amount of money to do whatever the contract is trying to achieve.

Getting Data vs Setting Data Functions

Our getter function for *message*, *message()* doesn't change anything since it simply 'views' data. *message()* is an example of calling a function that doesn't modify data at all. Such functions run instantly since it doesn't involve a transaction and doesn't need to mined.

But when we want to modify data stored in a contract, for example invoking *setMessage()*, we invoke it by sending a transaction to our contract instance targeting the *setMessage()* function. Note that anytime we submit a transaction to the network, it takes time to be processed. For example if we send money from one to another, the total time taken is about 30 seconds. Essentially, any time we want to change any data on the block chain, we have to submit a transaction and wait for the block that the transaction is in to be mined. The mining process first goes through the proof of work algorithm as covered in the previous chapter. After that, the new block has to be confirmed by other nodes. And we need a short gew seconds to return an answer back to the front end user interface (normally a website). The whole process can take anywhere from 15 to 30 seconds to execute.

Secondly, every time we send a transaction to a function, we are returned the transaction hash (see below).

The hash identifies the transaction that has just occurred and is unique for every transaction. We don't get a return value back even if we explicit add a *return* statement in our function. For example, the below *setMessage* function doesn't return *message* even though it has the *return* keyword.

```
function setMessage(string newMessage) public returns (string){
  message = newMessage;
  return message;
}
```

Third, sending a transaction to a function costs money. You can try it out on Remix on your own. In JavaScript VM environment, select an account with 100 ether and deploy the Greetings contract. You will notice that your account balance drops to 99.999... ether. If you call *setMessage* to update the value stored in the block chain. Your account balance drops slightly further (fig. 2.7).

Environment	JavaScript VM		
Account	0xca3...a733c (99.9999999999997349		
Gas limit	3000000		
Value	0	wei	

Figure 2.7

Both transactions incur very little ether but it did cost money to update the value there. Note that calling *setMessage* in Remix seems instantaneous. But if we execute these transactions on a public network (Main, Rineby, Kovan, Roysten networks), it will take around 15-30 seconds. This is the average time to have a new block mined and added onto the blockchain. But in our test network in the local browser, the blocktime gets tuned down to almost instantaneous.

So keep that in mind when we build apps that involve updating data, we have to wait 15-30 seconds for that data to be processed. So while we wait for a transaction to process, make sure we show some message like "you just submitted a transaction" or a loading icon.

In the next two sections, we discuss more about different units of ether and the concept of gas in

Ethereum.

Different Units of Ether

Beside the 'Value' field in Remix, there is a drop down where you can see options, wei, gwei, finney and ether which are different units of ether just as a hundred cents is to one dollar (fig. 2.8).

Figure 2.8

wei is a very small unit of ether. 1 ether = 1,000,000,000,000,000,000 wei. There is no smaller unit than wei. That is, you cannot have 0.5 wei.

If you google for 'wei converter', you will find many websites which let you easily convert between different units of measurement (fig. 2.9). But we usually work just with wei or ether.

Wei	1000000000000000000
Kwei, Ada, Femtoether	1000000000000000
Mwei, Babbage, Picoether	1000000000000
Gwei, Shannon, Nanoether, Nano	1000000000
Szabo, Microether,Micro	1000000
Finney, Milliether,Milli	1000
Ether	1
Kether, Grand,Einstein	0.001
Mether	0.000001
Gether	0.000000001
Tether	0.000000000001
USD(at 687.762$ p/ ether)	687.762
EUR(at 566.221€ p/ ether)	566.221

Figure 2.9 https://etherconverter.online/

Here are the denominations:
1 ether = 1000000000000000000 wei
1 ether = 1000000000000000 Kwei
1 ether = 1000000000000 Mwei
1 ether = 1000000000 Gwei
1 ether = 1000000 Szabo
1 ether = 1000 Finney
1 ether = 0.001 Kether
1 ether = 0.000001 Mether
1 ether = 0.000000001 Gether
1 ether = 0.000000000001 Tether

Gas

Gas in Ethereum is a unit of measurement for computational steps. It measures how much work we are executing with our code. Every transaction is required to include a gas limit and a fee that it is willing to pay per gas. It is similar to how you have to pay Amazon some money to run your code on Amazon web services. If you code requires more computational steps, the more money you have to pay Amazon.

Running of the smart contracts is done by a miner, who spends their own time, electricity and computing hardware to execute the codes and finalize the transaction. Different kinds of transaction require different amounts of gas to complete. For example, an add operation consumes 3 gas and a multiplication operation consumes 5 gas.

Whenever we issue a transaction that modifies the blockchain, we have to specify two properties in our transaction object:

Gas Price: amount of wei the sender is willing to pay per unit gas to get this transaction processed. e.g. If I offer gas price of 10, that means I am willing to pay 10 * 3 wei for an addition operation. *Gas Limit*: total units of gas that we are willing to spend at most with this transaction.

So, note especially if we have a *for* loop that loops over a collection of records that might grow or shrink over time. Can we possibly use a different data structure to avoid loops? For example, using mapping/hashtable instead of an array to store data? We will study optimizing code to avoid incurring more gas in the sections where we develop advanced smart contracts.

If we execute more gas than the *gasLimit*, the execution of the function immediately halts. The remnant gas that is not spent is sent back to the person who created the transaction object. You only spend the gas that is actually consumed by the operations executed by your contract.

Because we have to spend some amount of gas to store/modify data in our contract, it can have a limiting effect on the kinds of applications we can develop. Suppose we want to create a Decentralized application version of Twitter that allow users to post tweets that are stored on the blockchain. The user than has to pay money to post a tweet! Considering that there is already a free version of Twitter, would they want to still pay to post a tweet? However, in certain situations, this is exactly what users might want.

For example, a country might censor/control certain centralized social media applications using Firewall. However, they are unable to censor out a decentralized app which stores data on the blockchain since a copy of the blockchain is stored on each Ethereum node. And users don't mind paying to post Tweets on such a blockchain to by pass censorship.

Summary

In this chapter, we were introduced to writing a smart contract with the Solidity programming language. We wrote our first smart contract using the online Remix editor and learnt how to initialise a smart contract and call functions on it. We went through simple testing of the contract and the differences between getter and setter functions. In the next chapter, we will go through compiling a smart contract apart from Remix with *solc*, and unit testing with Mocha and Ganache.

The source code in this chapter can be found at: https://github.com/greglim81/solidity-chapter2

CHAPTER 3: COMPILING WITH SOLC, UNIT TESTING WITH MOCHA & GANACHE

Eventually, we want to deploy our contract onto the main or test network so that we can use this contract with a user frontend to form a full DApp. To do so, we first need to deploy the contract byte code to the network. Remember that the Solidity compiler spits out both the contract byte code and ABI.

Although Remix is great, it's limited to the browser. To write automated tests and the React front end, we will eventually have to write smart contract code in our own editor. Also, Remix doesn't link to GitHub or any version control to allow us to share our contract code.

Thus in this chapter, we will begin using our own code editor to write our contracts. We will be putting together a custom Node.js project from scratch that will aid us in contract creation, local testing and deployment to the Rinkeby network and in the process understand how the deployment process works. This will also help us to understand what other smart contract deployment tools like Truffle, web3 and other libraries are doing behind the scenes.

In this chapter, we will setup our Solidity compiler which outputs our:
1) ABI that we use to work with Javascript to create our front end user interface and
2) byte code that we deploy to the network

We will also conduct unit testing for our Greetings smart contract. Although we can manually test our contracts on Remix, we need automated test sets for more complicated contracts to make sure that our contract is working the way we expect as huge amounts of money are involved in smart contract transactions. Unit testing for smart contracts are the more important than for normal apps because of the huge monetary transactions involved. In this chapter, we show how unit testing is done for our simple Greetings contract which will provide us the foundations for unit testing on more complicated contracts.

We will make use of the Mocha test library for unit testing. If you have not worked with Mocha before, it's a JavaScript generic testing framework that can be used with all kinds of Javascript projects.

Begin we carry on, make sure you're running at least version 8.0.0 of Node JS. You can check your current version by running the command *node -v* in your command line. If you are running an older version, you can easily update it at: https://nodejs.org/en/download/.

Creating our Greetings Node Project

In Terminal, go to the location where you want to store all Ethereum projects and create a new directory 'Greetings'. Go to 'Greetings' and generate a new Node project by running 'npm init'. Press enter for the next series of questions.

When you are done, a package.json will be generated in the directory.

Next, open the project folder in your code editor of choice. In this book, I will be using the VS Code editor.

Overview of 'Greetings' Project directory

Our 'Greetings' project directory will eventually consist of the following:

contracts (folder containing our Solidity contract source code file, can contain more than one contract)
-    Greetings.sol
test (folder containing our test scripts written in Mocha code)
-    Greetings.test.js
package.json (file to record different dependencies installed in our project)
compile.js (script file to compile each of the contracts inside 'contracts' directory)
deploy.js (deployment file to Ethereum network)

So in the Greetings project directory, create the *contracts* and *test* folders. In *contracts* folder, create a new file Greetings.sol and copy the Greetings contract code from chapter two into it.

Compile.js

We will first work on compile.js file because deploy.js and Greetings.test.js depends on a compiled contract.

First, we will install the Solidity compiler node module. In Terminal, run the following command:

```
npm install --save solc
```

solc is the Solidity compiler provided by Ethereum to compile *.sol* files.

Next, in the project root directory, create a new file compile.js with the following code:

```
const path = require('path');
const greetingsPath =path.resolve(__dirname,'contracts','Greetings.sol');

const fs = require('fs');
const solc = require('solc');

const source = fs.readFileSync(greetingsPath, 'utf8');
```

```
console.log(solc.compile(source,1));
```

Code Explanation

```
const path = require('path');
```

The *path* Node.js module helps build a directory path to our Greetings.sol file.

__dirname is a constant defined by Node.js which returns us the current working directory which is our *Greetings* folder directory.

```
const greetingsPath =path.resolve(__dirname,'contracts','Greetings.sol');
```

We then pass *__dirname*, 'contracts' and 'Greetings.sol' arguments in our call to *path.resolve* to point directly to Greetings.sol file in 'contracts' folder. We call *path.resolve* instead of hardcoding our path to give us cross platform compatibility so that we can run this compile script either on Windows or Unix based system.

```
// fs module provides an API for interacting with file system
const fs = require('fs');
const solc = require('solc');

const source = fs.readFileSync(greetingsPath, 'utf8');
console.log(solc.compile(source,1));
```

With *fs.readFileSync*, we read in the contents of Greetings.sol, our raw Solidity source code. We then compile it with *solc.compile(source,1)*. The argument '1' represents the number of contracts to compile. Also notice that we are logging the compiled results to the console. This is because we want to illustrate examples of compiled bytecode and ABI code.

Running Compile.js

To run compile.js, in Terminal in project directory, run:
```
node compile.js
```

You should see a lot of data being logged:

```
{ contracts:
   { ':Greetings':
      { assembly: [Object],
        bytecode: '608060405234801561001057600080fd5b5060405161...
```

Notice in the console output an object with *contracts* property, which contains all the contracts compiled by our Solidity compiler. In our case, it is the 'Greetings' contract. Under 'Greetings', you see several other key-value pairs (e.g. *functionHashes*, *gasEstimates*, *interface*, *metadata*, *opcodes* etc). The ones which we care about are *bytecode* and *interface*. *bytecode* is the actual bytecode we deploy on the Ethereum blockchain.

The other property we are interested is *interface* which is the contract ABI. Remember that the ABI is essentially the communication layer between Solidity and JavaScript. If you look at the value, it really just lists out all the different functions that exist on the contract (see below) that can be called. It also specifies how many arguments, what type of arguments, what return type and values are associated with each of those functions.

```
[
        {
                "constant": false,
                "inputs": [
                        {
                                "name": "newMessage",
                                "type": "string"
                        }
                ],
                "name": "setMessage",
                "outputs": [],
                "payable": false,
                "stateMutability": "nonpayable",
                "type": "function"
        },
        {
                "constant": true,
                "inputs": [],
                "name": "message",
                "outputs": [
                        {
                                "name": "",
                                "type": "string"
                        }
                ],
                "payable": false,
                "stateMutability": "view",
                "type": "function"
        },
        {
                "inputs": [
                        {
                                "name": "initialMessage",
                                "type": "string"
                        }
                ],
                "payable": false,
                "stateMutability": "nonpayable",
                "type": "constructor"
        }
```

]

Finally, to make our compiler accessible to other files, we will change the last line of compile.js to:

```
module.exports = solc.compile(source, 1).contracts[':Greetings'];
```

Unit Testing

Having compiled our contract we will start testing it. Remember that it's important to do so because contracts work with a lot of money.

We will write tests that directly call different functions in our contract. We will take our bytecode and deploy our contract to a local test Ethereum network running on our own laptop/desktop solely for deploying and testing our contract. This is something that we've been already doing with Remix.

We will create our local test network with a library called Ganache. TestRPC is the old name of the library which was later renamed as Ganache.

We will take the ABI Javascript interface and feed that into the web3 library. Web3 is a library to get programmatic access to a deployed contract on the blockchain.

Installation of Modules for Testing

To prepare for testing, we're going to install a couple of modules using *npm*.

Installation

First, we will install the testing framework Mocha, Ganache CLI and web3 by running the command:

```
npm install --save mocha ganache-cli web3@1.0.0-beta.34
```

(at time of writing, this book uses the 1.0.0-beta.34 version of web3)

Back in our app directory, in *test* folder (create a 'test' folder if you have not already done so), create a file called Greetings.test.js. In this file, we will write code to make some testing assertions about our deployed contract. Assertions verify that things are correct. They make it easier to test our code so we don't have to perform thousands of *if* statements. Fill in the following code into Greetings.test.js:

Greetings.test.js

```
const assert = require('assert');
const ganache = require('ganache-cli');
const Web3 = require('web3');
```

```
const web3 = new Web3(ganache.provider());
```

Code Explanation

```
const assert = require('assert');
```

asset is a standard library in Node.js. It's used to make test assertions i.e., some variable is equal to some value.

```
const ganache = require('ganache-cli');
```

ganache serves as our local Ethereum network.

```
const Web3 = require('web3');
```

Notice that *assert* and *ganache* are lower case, but *Web3* is uppercase. When we use *Web3*, we first require a constructor function, and *Web3* is a constructor used to creates instances of the web3 library. Because *Web3* is a constructor function, by convention, we capitalise it.

```
const web3 = new Web3(ganache.provider());
```

With the *Web3* constructor, we then create an instance of *web3*. A *web3* instance connects to a node in the Etheruem network (you can establish connections with multiple nodes with multiple *web3* instances). By specifying *ganache.provider* into the *Web3* constructor, we are telling this new web3 instance to connect to the *ganache* local test network that we are hosting on our machine. In future, when we provide to a different test work like Rinkeby, we will replace this provider with a different provider that will link us up to those other networks.

Quick Overview of Mocha

Mocha is a general testing framework that can be used to test any type of JavaScript code we want, whether it's a normal or Ethereum based application. Before we go on with testing, we have to be familiar with a few Mocha functions:

it

The *it* function runs one individual test and makes an assertion for example, we have a value our code produces and another value that we think should be equal to that. We then compare the two values together and make sure that the value outputted is what we expect to be. We refer to that as an *assertion*.

describe

The *describe* function groups together one or more *it* functions. *describe* is really just organization in nature to help us group together certain functions which are testing the same thing.

beforeEach

The *beforeEach* function executes some general setup code for *it* functions. It acts as a utility function used to extract some amount of logic common to a lot of our test. For example, if we have multiple *it* functions that does a similar set of logic, we could use a *beforeEach* function to run that logic instead of having the same code replicated in each *it* function.

package.json

Before we begin, make the following changes to package.json:

```
"scripts": {
  "test": "mocha"
}
```

Thus, when we execute '*npm run test*', we will be running the *mocha* command. Mocha will load our Greetings.test.js and start to execute the tests that we have specified.

Fetching of Accounts from Ganache

We will now access web3 and use it to retrieve a list of accounts automatically created for us in the local Ganache network. Remember that we need an account to deploy a contract.

Back in Greetings.test.js, add in the below codes in **bold** to define our *beforeEach* statement:

```
const assert = require('assert');
const ganache = require('ganache-cli');
const Web3 = require('web3');

const web3 = new Web3(ganache.provider());

beforeEach(() => {
    web3.eth.getAccounts()
    .then(fetchedAccounts => {
        console.log(fetchedAccounts);
    });
});

describe('Greetings',() => {
    it('dummy test', () => {
```

```
    });
});
```

Code Explanation

```
beforeEach(() => {
    web3.eth.getAccounts()
    .then(fetchedAccounts => {
        console.log(fetchedAccounts);
    });
});
```

The Ganache module (*ganache.provider()*) automatically creates a set of accounts in the local Ganache test network. We can freely send or receive ether from these accounts for testing purposes. The above code retrieves these set of accounts.

web3 contains an *eth* object (*web3.eth*) specifically for Ethereum blockchain interactions. *web3.eth.getAccounts()* returns us the list of test accounts. The *web3* library has many different modules to be used for different types of cryptocurrency. We are accessing one particular module 'eth'. We then access the *getAccounts* function from the 'eth' module.

Almost anything we do with web3 is asynchronous in nature and that means it will always be returning a promise. For example, *getAccounts* returns a promise with the list of accounts. We then use the *then* statement to subscribe to the promise and print the list of accounts returned.

```
describe('Greetings',() => {
    it('dummy test', () => {

    });
});
```

The *it* function is used to custom test different aspects of the contract which we will use in detail later. For now, our *it* function doesn't do anything, we simply include so that *beforeEach* is called.

Running our Test File

Now, let's save this and run it to make sure that the list of accounts is properly fetched.

Remember to make a small change in package.json file if you have not:

```
"scripts":{
  "test":"mocha"
}
```

In terminal, run:

npm run test

In the test run, you should see a listing of ten separate accounts like:

```
[ '0x23Db338d638aa05B6Ae0B74c7D8C36f655c38Ca5',
  '0x9340425E0B15BBe1CAB1690B816D8ade86Dcc7bC',
  '0x042445D630b8a0802b7a7Bbb3cB17548a089284b',
  '0xac69BED1884B29D9557ECFAabe80f2425946f0C4',
  '0x89B26f656402D0b44aA467cF89E81Ac2202106e1',
  '0x30C5e18eFFDF0bD523bd8353b5469e89a06723f8',
  '0x493baBeD4772770aea00dCA788bA593651ACCcD0',
  '0x1469B3D5e314cE2AA9295AcFEDd3f63D7780E84D',
  '0xeBeaDF25d7D34695FF7c5706Ec3Ee880Bc4E6d92',
  '0xeffa25a82Ef5555645b296f6B7924B49F50169c2' ]
```

These are pre-generated accounts created by the Ganache local test network. We can use any of them to deploy contracts to send ether or call a function on a contract. This makes it easier for us since we don't have to create an account every time we want to run a test.

Refactoring to async/await

Because anything we do with web3 is asynchronous in nature, and the code to handle promises can be difficult for some who are not used to writing callbacks, we use the *await* keyword to make our code to handle asynchronous calls easier. We can change our *beforeEach* code to the following:

Greetings.test.js

```
beforeEach(async () => {
    accounts = await web3.eth.getAccounts();
    console.log(accounts);
});
```

The *await* keyword waits for asynchronous calls to complete successfully before carrying on code execution. So, it resembles 'normal' synchronous function calls. Note that when we use *await*, we have to mark the function with the *async* keyword to mean that the function contained in it is asynchronous in nature.

Smart Contract Deployment to Ganache with web3

So far, we have only been testing our retrieval of accounts from Ganache. We have not yet deployed and tested our contract in the Ganache network. To do so, we first need to deploy our contract to the

Ganache network. We will do so using web3. Add the following codes in **bold**:

Greetings.test.js

```
const assert = require('assert');
const ganache = require('ganache-cli');
const Web3 = require('web3');

const web3 = new Web3(ganache.provider());

const { interface,bytecode } = require('../compile');

let accounts;
let greetings

beforeEach(async () => {
    accounts = await web3.eth.getAccounts();
    greetings = await new web3.eth.Contract(JSON.parse(interface))
    .deploy({ data: bytecode, arguments: ['Hello World'] })
    .send({from: accounts[0], gas:'1000000'})
});
```

Code Explanation

```
const { interface,bytecode } = require('../compile');
```

For deployment, we will need the ABI interface and compiled bytecode of our smart contract. The two are taken from the *interface* and *bytecode* properties of the compiled smart contract object which is the output of compile.js.

```
greetings = await new web3.eth.Contract(JSON.parse(interface))
```

The *Contract* property of *eth* library is a constructor function that allows us to access existing contracts on the block chain or to deploy new contracts. It takes the contract ABI as argument and returns the contract object. *interface* is our ABI - the interface between our Solidity world and JavaScript. Because ABI is in a JSON representation, we use *JSON.parse* so that we pass in an actual JavaScript object. Because creating a contract is asynchronous, we use the *await* keyword.

```
.deploy({ data: bytecode, arguments: ['Hello World'] })
.send({from: accounts[0], gas:'1000000'})
```

Next, we call the *deploy* function of our *Contract* instance to deploy a copy of this contract. We create a transaction object that has the *data* property which holds the actual deployed bytecode and *arguments* property which is a list of arguments to pass into the constructor function of the contract.

We then pass in this transaction object to *deploy* which still doesn't actually deploy anything. It just starts to create an object that can then be deployed to the network. It's the *send* method that actually triggers the transaction to deploy the contract to the network.

In *send*, the *from* property is the person or account that is being used to create the contract. In our case, we will use *account[0]* (the first account) to deploy the contract. For a transaction to create a contract, we leave the *to* field blank.

We also specify the amount of gas that can be used up with `gas:'1000000'`. There are other properties in the transaction object that we can specify but are optional like *value*, *gasPrice*, *nonce*.

Accessing a Deployed Contract

We can also use web3 to get access to contracts that have already been deployed to the network. We will similarly need it's ABI to interact with it via JavaScrpt and also the address of the specific deployed contract. (All deployed contracts have their own unique address to identify it in the blockchain). When interacting with an existing deployed contract, we don't need to specify the byte code.

Asserting Deployment

In this section, we will write some meaningful tests on our simple deployed contract. Although we are testing our simple 'Hello World' Greetings contract, you will be using the same steps and procedure when you move on to more complicated contracts.

First, add the following codes in bold into Greetings.test.ts as shown below:

Greetings.test.js

```
const assert = require('assert');
const ganache = require('ganache-cli');
const Web3 = require('web3');

const web3 = new Web3(ganache.provider());

const { interface,bytecode } = require('../compile');

let accounts;
let greetings

beforeEach(async () => {
    accounts = await web3.eth.getAccounts();
    greetings = await new web3.eth.Contract(JSON.parse(interface))
    .deploy({ data: bytecode, arguments: ['Hello World'] })
```

```
    .send({from: accounts[0], gas:'1000000'})
});

describe('Greetings',() => {
    it('deploys a greetings contract', () => {
      console.log(greetings);
      assert.ok(greetings.options.address);
    });
});
```

This tests to see if our greetings contract was successfully deployed.

```
greetings.options.address
```

greetings which hold the reference to our *greetings* contract instance has an *options* property which has the *address* property which holds the address of where we deployed the contract.

The *assert.ok* method makes some assertion that whatever we are passing into the function is a value that exists. That is, we assert that *greetings.options.address* is a defined value. If *greetings.options.address* does not exist, then this test will fail. But if there is any value, then the test will pass.

So run *npm run test* and you should see something like the below in the Terminal:

✓ *deploys a greetings contract*

1 passing (220ms)

It is useful to always start off with a simple test like this to make sure that the deployment process is working correctly.

Additional tests to assert initial value of message

In this section, we add two further tests to check that there is a default message when the contract is instantiated and that the message is correctly changed when *setMessage* function is called on the contract.

Add the following codes in bold into the describe block for the two tests:

```
describe('Greetings',() => {
    it('deploys a greetings contract', () => {
      console.log(greetings);
      assert.ok(greetings.options.address);
    });

    it('has a default message', async () => {
```

44

```
        const message = await greetings.methods.message().call();
        assert.equal(message, 'Hello World')
    });

    it('can change the message',async () =>{
        await greetings.methods.setMessage('Hello Avengers').send({ from:
accounts[0] } )
        const message = await greetings.methods.message().call();
        assert.equal(message,'Hello Avengers');
    });
});
```

Code Explanation

```
    it('has a default message', async () => {
        const message = await greetings.methods.message().call();
```

The above *it* function tests that there is a default *message* value 'Hello World' when the contract is first instantiated. *greetings.methods* is an object that contains all of the different public functions that exist in our contract. e.g. *methods.setMessage(…)* We use *greetings.methods.message().call()* to call *message()* to retrieve *message* value.

Note that calling the method *message()* is asynchronous, thus we have to use *await* to wait for *message()* method call to send us back the value.

```
        assert.equal(message, 'Hello World')
    });
```

After retrieving *message*, we assert that the value in *message* is the same as the value given to the constructor i.e. 'Hello World'.

```
    it('can change the message',async () =>{
        await greetings.methods.setMessage('Hello Avengers').send({ from:
accounts[0] } )
        const message = await greetings.methods.message().call();
        assert.equal(message,'Hello Avengers');
    });
```

For the second *it* function, we first call *setMessage* with the string 'Hello Avengers'. A very important note is that instead of using *call()*, we use *send()* because we need to send a transaction to modify data. We also need to specify in *send()* which account is sending this transaction with *from: accounts[0]*. In our case, we use the first account provided by Ganache to do so.

Running our Test

Run *npm run test* to run the tests. If the tests pass, it means we are getting a default message set on this instance and also that the contract has successfully changed the message. So I hope you notice the pattern of unit testing, that is, we deploy a contract, manipulate in some fashion, and then make assertions through the *it* function blocks. We repeat this for different functions of the contract

In the next chapter, we will work on deploying our contract to the Rinkeby test network. The process of deploying to the Rinkeby network is the same as deploying to the main network. We obviously deploy to the Rinkeby network for now because we have to use real money to deploy on the main network.

Summary

In this chapter, we create our own compile script with the Solidity compiler *solc*. We learnt how to access the compiled byte code and ABI interface which will come in useful later when we communicate our smart contract with React. We also began unit testing our contract with the Mocha test framework and the Ganache test network. In the next chapter, we will begin deploying our contract to an actual test network.

The source code for this chapter can be located at: https://github.com/greglim81/solidity-chapter3and4

Chapter 4: Deploying Smart Contracts to Test/Main Networks

Before we can deploy our smart contract to a test or main network, we need to have with us our twelve word mnemonic which MetaMask provided for us when we signed up for an account back in chapter one. Now, we will go into the detail on the use of the twelve word mnemonic.

For each Ethereum account, we have an address, a public key and a private key. These information can be hard to remember and there is also a possibility one might lose it. To resolve this issue, the Ethereum community have came up with a twelve random word mnemonic that allows us to automatically generate a series of different accounts with a public key, private key and address. This is the twelve word mnemonic provided to us by MetaMask.

We can feed these twelve words into a BIP39 mnemonic algorithm which outputs a series of different accounts each of which have their own public key, private key and address. Behind the scenes, this is what the MetaMask extension is doing for us.

Getting More Ether

Before we start developing more complex contracts, we need to get some ether to work on the Rinkeby test network. Currently, we don't even have enough ether on the Rinkeby network to deploy a contract. Remember that doing transactions and function computations cost some amount of ether. You can check how much ether you have on a specific network by going to MetaMask and selecting the specific network (fig. 4.1).

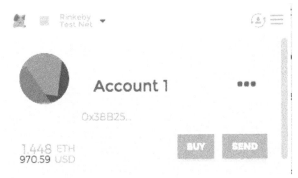

Figure 4.1

To request for more ether for testing purposes on the Rinkeby network, go to faucet.rinkeby.io and go through the instructions on the site. Essentially, it's to paste your Ethereum address on one social media platform to avoid malicious users who spam the test network.

47

Deployment with INFURA

In the coming sections, we will use our account that has some amount of ether on the test network and also the twelve word mnemonic phrase in our deployment script.

To deploy our contract, we will need to connect to a node in the Rinkeby network. We can run an Ethereum node in our own machine that connects to the Rinkeby network. However, setting up our own Ethereum node can be difficult, takes a lot of time and of course, we have to provide our own hardware, electricity etc. INFURA eliminates the requirement to install, configure and maintain Ethereum nodes for Ethereum Dapp developers. INFURA is a public API that provides an easy way to deploy and access a node hosted on the Rinkeby, Ropsten, Kovan and main network.

INFURA Signup

At time of writing, INFURA is free. Go to infura.io, click on 'Get Started For Free' and register for an access token which is the API key that we need (fig. 4.2).

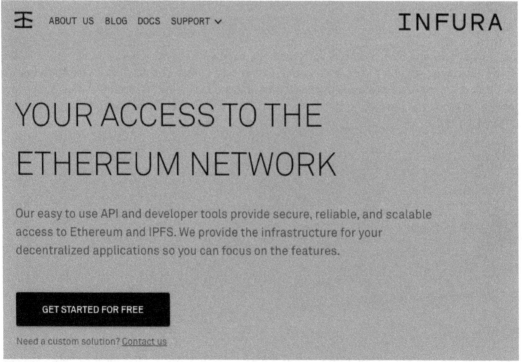

Figure 4.2

Once you have signed up, an email with your unique API link will be sent to you.

Wallet Provider Setup

Next, we need to install a special provider called the HD Wallet-enabled provider. The HD Wallet-enabled provider allows us to sign transactions for addresses derived from our 12-word mnemonic

Run the following in Terminal:

```
npm install --save truffle-hdwallet-provider
```

Creating our Deploy Script

In this section, we will create a deploy script to deploy our smart contract onto the main/test network. In our project directory, create a new file deploy.js with the following codes:

```
const HDWalletProvider = require('truffle-hdwallet-provider');
const Web3 = require('web3');
const { interface,bytecode} = require('./compile');

const provider = new HDWalletProvider(
  'please kindly insert your own twelve word memnonic from meta mask
here',
  'https://rinkeby.infura.io/<as sent by infura to your email>'
);

const web3 = new Web3(provider);
```

Code Explanation

```
const HDWalletProvider = require('truffle-hdwallet-provider');
const Web3 = require('web3');
```

HDWalletProvider allow us to specify which account to deploy our contract from our twelve word mnemonic.

```
const { interface,bytecode} = require('./compile');
```

As discussed earlier, we import *interface* and *bytecode* properties from our compile script

```
const provider = new HDWalletProvider(
  'please kindly insert your own twelve word mnemonic from meta mask
here',
  'https://rinkeby.infura.io/hdsklfkhdjsgflsf'
```

```
);
```

The first argument to *HDWalletProvider* constructor is our MetaMask account mnemonic used to derive our public/private key. If you forget your mnemonic, go to MetaMask and create a new account. Because this deployment script is used only by yourself, we can be safe about using our twelve word mnemonic here. Make sure that you don't pass this deployment to script to others before removing your twelve word mnemonic.

The second argument is the url link of the Ethereum network we want to connect to. In our case, we paste the link from the email received from INFURA.

```
const web3 = new Web3(provider);
```

We then instantiate our web3 instance with the INFURA provider. We can use this web3 instance to send ether, deploy contracts, update contracts and also on.

Deployment to Rinkeby

Our deploy.js code will look similar to Greetings.test.js. Add the following codes into deploy.js:

deploy.js

```
const deploy = async () => {
    accounts = await web3.eth.getAccounts();

    console.log('attempting to deploy from account',accounts[0]);

    const result = await new web3.eth.Contract(JSON.parse(interface))
      .deploy({data: '0x' + bytecode, arguments:['Hello World']})
      .send({gas: '1000000', from: accounts[0] });

    console.log('Contract deployed to', result.options.address);
}

deploy();
```

(*As of time of writing, do note that you have to append '0x' before *bytecode* in *data* property to avoid an error while deployment)

Code Explanation

```
    accounts = await web3.eth.getAccounts();
```

Just like what we have done in Greetings.test.js, we first get a list of accounts from our web3 instance.

50

```
console.log('attempting to deploy from account',accounts[0]);
```

We print out the address the account used to deploy this contract. This will prove useful later when we track deployment progress of our contract on Etherscan.

```
const result = await new web3.eth.Contract(JSON.parse(interface))
```

We provide the ABI *interface* property into the web3 *Contract* constructor to create an instance of our contract.

```
console.log('Contract deployed to', result.options.address);
```

Lastly, we log to console *result.options.address* so that we know our deployed contract address.

Running deploy.js

To run deploy.js, in Terminal run: *node deploy.js*

It will take some amount of time for the contract creation transaction to occur on Rinkeby network due to mining, proof of work algorithm etc. After that, you should see the address of your deployed contract logged in the console.

This is where the contract exists on the Rinkeby test network. This is useful to us to build our HTML/CSS/JS frontend to interact with this contract. In the next chapter, we will write a more advanced smart contract, deploy it in the same fashion and learn how to interact with it from a React JS frontend.

Observing Deployment on Etherscan

To observe deployment of your Contract on the Rinkeby network, go to rinkeby.etherscan.io. Etherscan (etherscan.io) is a website that reads all transactions that flow into the Kovan, Ropsten, Rinkeby test and main networks. You can search by account addresses and also deployed contracts. So if you grab your address from Terminal, and paste it in the search bar of rinkeby.etherscan.io, it will show you the deployment details about your contract.

You can see the transaction hash used to deploy the contract, the block number, age of the contract, the account used to deploy the contract and so on (fig. 4.3). We can also see the list of transactions that have been sent to this contract. The contract byte code is also publicly available at the site.

Figure 4.3

Summary

In preparation to deploy to a test network, we first got more ether for our account in the test network. We deployed our contract through the INFURA API to give us access to an Ethereum node without having to host one ourselves. In the process, we created our own deploy script. We finally observed deployment of our contract on Etherscan.

Once again, the code for this chapter can be located at:
https://github.com/greglim81/solidity-chapter3and4

CHAPTER 5: EBAY SMART CONTRACT

In this chapter, we will focus on developing a real life use case smart contract which will allow us to create a simplified eBay clone. Our app will allow sellers to post product/services for sale and buyers transfer ethers to the sellers to purchase their products and services.

Sellers will post whatever products/services they would like to offer for sale at a specific price in ethers. Buyers can then click on the individual product/service to buy them, and our smart contract will transfer the specified ether from the buyer to the seller. A transaction will be logged in the blockchain to verify that the buy/sell transaction has indeed happened from buyer A to seller B.

Contract Code

We first show the full code of our smart contract before explaining it in depth in the following sections. You can get a copy of it at: https://github.com/greglim81/solidity-chapter5/

EbayClone.sol

```
pragma Solidity ^0.4.23;

contract EBayClone {
    struct Product {
        uint id;
        address seller;
        address buyer;
        string name;
        string description;
        uint price;
    }

    uint productCounter;
    mapping (uint => Product) public products;

    function sellProduct(string _name, string _description, uint _price)
public{
        Product memory newProduct = Product({
            id: productCounter,
            seller: msg.sender,
            buyer: 0x0,
            name: _name,
            description: _description,
            price: _price
        });
```

```
        products[productCounter] = newProduct;
        productCounter++;
    }

    function getNumberOfProducts() public view returns (uint) {
        return productCounter;
    }

    function buyProduct (uint _id) payable public{
      Product storage product = products[_id];
      require(product.buyer == 0x0);
      require(msg.sender != product.seller);
      require(msg.value == product.price);
      product.buyer = msg.sender;
      product.seller.transfer(msg.value);
    }
}
```

Code Explanation

Solidity provides a way to define new types in the form of structs. In the following example: we define a struct *Product* to define our Product with the following code:

```
struct Product {
    uint id;
    address seller;
    address buyer;
    string name;
    string description;
    uint price;
}
```

id contains the product id. *seller* contains the address of the seller of the product. *buyer* contains the address of the buyer of the product and is initially blank. It will only be populated when a buyer buys this product. *seller* and *buyer* both are of type *address*. *address* is a type in Solidity that stores addresses. It has methods tied to it for sending money as we shall see later.

Quick Introduction to Variable Types in Solidity

name, *description* and *price* fields should be self-explanatory. Just like many other programming languages, Solidity offers many basic variable types like *string* (sequence of characters), *bool* (boolean value), *int8*, *int16*, *int32*...*int256* (the number after the word 'int' specifies the number of bits used to store the number, how large a number it can contain e.g. *int8*: -128 to 127, *int16*: -32,768 to 32767 etc.). You also have uint which is an unsigned integer, meaning that it can only store positive numbers without decimal. We use this for *price* since price cannot be negative. To store decimal numbers, you can use *fixed* or *ufixed*.

Internal Data Structure

```
uint productCounter;
mapping (uint => Product) public products;
```

Our contract will also have two fields, *productCounter* and *products*. *productCounter* provides the value of the next product id. It will begin from 0 for the first product, and then subsequently be incremented by 1 for each new product being put on sale.

The data structure holding all the products is a *mapping* type which is a hash table of key-value pairs: key being product *id* and value being our *Product* struct.

It would be something like:
0 – product 1
1 – product 2
2 – product 3
3 – product 4
…

With a hashtable, given a product id, we can retrieve our requested *Product* immediately. This is very important in terms of algorithmic efficiency. If we do not use a hashtable but instead use an array, to retrieve a Product given a product id, we would have to loop through the entire array and compare each Product's id to see if that's the Product we want. If the array size is *n*, we would take *n* steps for Product retrieval as compared to retrieval in a hashtable which is just 1 step. And this is even more important because to run operations in smart contracts, remember that we have to pay more amounts of gas for more operations. And this is why algorithm efficiency is important especially in Ethereum.

As a side note, although our mapping is (*uint => Product*), we can have mappings involving other variable types for example:

```
mapping(string => string)
mapping(int => bool)
```

Our Smart Contract Functions

We would next have three functions in our smart contract: *sellProduct*, *buyProduct* and *getNumberOfProducts*. All three functions are declared as *public* to allow anyone to call these functions.

sellProduct

```
    function sellProduct(string _name, string _description, uint _price)
public{
        Product memory newProduct = Product({
            id: productCounter,
            seller: msg.sender,
            buyer: 0x0,
            name: _name,
            description: _description,
            price: _price
        });

        products[productCounter] = newProduct;
        productCounter++;
    }
```

sellProduct will take in arguments *name*, *description* and *price* as inputted by the user of our application. With these values, we will create a new Product object *newProduct*. The *memory* keyword tells Solidity to create a chunk of space for *newProduct* at method runtime, guaranteeing its size and structure for future use in that method.

msg

We set *id* of *newProduct* to be *productCounter* and *seller* to be *msg.sender*.

```
        seller: msg.sender,
```

But where does *msg* come from since we have not declared it any in our contract?

msg here is a global object variable with properties that describe who called this function and also details about the transaction the function call came from. The *msg* object is available whenever we create a contract or any function invokation. *msg* has the following properties:

msg.data : 'data' field from the call or transaction that invoked the current function e.g. for contract creation, it is the contract source code. For a function invocation, it refers to the arguments that we send to that function

msg.gas: amount of gas the current function invocation has available

msg.sender: address of the account that started the current function invocation

msg.value: amount of wei sent along with the function invocation

Back in our *sellProduct* function, *msg.sender* will return us the address of the seller. We thus assign *msg.sender* to *seller*.

```
        buyer: 0x0,
```

We set *buyer* to be blank by assigning it the value *0x0* (*buyer* will be assigned later when another user calls *buyProduct*). We then store *newProduct* into *products* hashtable with *productCounter* as key. Lastly, we increment *productCounter*.

buyProduct

Our *buyProduct* function will consists of the following code:

```
    function buyProduct (uint _id) payable public{
      Product storage product = products[_id];
      require(product.buyer == 0x0);
      require(msg.sender != product.seller); // buyer cannot be same as
seller
      require(msg.value == product.price);
      product.buyer = msg.sender;
      product.seller.transfer(msg.value);
  }
```

A user will call *buyProduct* with the product id she wish to buy as argument. Note that there is a *payable* keyword in the method header. It means that anyone who calls this function has to send some amount of ether along when calling this function.

We retrieve the value of ether sent through *msg.value*. From the caller's point of view, the sending of ether is done through specifying the *value* property. More on this later when we show you how to call this function.

```
    Product storage product = products[_id];
```

Next, we retrieve the product by specifying the id as key to the *products* hashtable.

```
      require(product.buyer == 0x0);
      require(msg.sender != product.seller); // buyer cannot be same as
seller
      require(msg.value == product.price);
```

Next, we have a series of *require* statements. *require* statements are requirements which have to be satisfied before code execution in the function can continue. That is, we pass in some required Boolean expression. If the Boolean expression is false, code execution will just stop and no changes are made to the contract. If the expression evaluates to true, code execution continues as usual.

The first *require* requires that the buyer of the product is 0x0, i.e. buyer has not been assigned which means that the product has not been bought. The second require requires that the buyer must be different from the seller. A seller can't buy its own product. Third, the value of ether sent in this method call must be equal to the product price. That is, you cannot buy this product at a discount or at a premium. Value sent has to be equal to product price.

Now, we can of course enforce these rules in the website user interface layer by auto filling values, filtering out products which have already been bought, or filtering out products which you are selling, but what if someone calls our smart contract directly bypassing the UI layer? So that is why we need the require statements in the smart contract itself.

```
product.buyer = msg.sender;
```

We assign caller of *buyProduct* to be the buyer of this product.

```
product.seller.transfer(msg.value);
```

And we transfer the value of ether from buyer to seller. Remember that seller is of *address* type. *address* provides us a collection of different methods to work with this address. We can send some money to this address by calling its *transfer()* method. So the code *product.seller.transfer(20)* will take some money from current account and send 20 wei to the address value of *product.seller*. That is, wei is deducted from the person invoking the *transfer* method, which in our case is the buyer.

address type also provides us with the *balance* property which you can use to check the balance of the address.

getNumberOfProducts

```
function getNumberOfProducts() public view returns (uint) {
    return productCounter;
}
```

Lastly, we have the *getNumberOfProducts* function which simply returns the current value of *productCounter*. We need the number of products later when we attempt to create an array of the same size to render the products in our React user frontend.

Testing our EBayClone in Remix

We will first test our contract in Remix. In Remix, make sure that your Environment is set to 'Javascript VM'. Copy and paste the EbayClone.sol code inside it. Compile, and click on 'Create' to create an instance of our smart contract that we can interact with and you should have the available functions to call (fig. 5.1).

Figure 5.1

If you click on *getNumberOfProducts*, you should have 0 printed in the Remix console.

```
{
        "0": "uint256: 0"
}
```

Now try calling *sellProduct* with the arguments "watch","sports watch", 20. Remember to include the double quotes for *name* and *description* into the input field in Remix. We specify 20 for the price which represent 20 wei (not 20 ethers!).

Now if you click on *getNumberOfProducts* again, you should have 1 printed.

```
{
        "0": "uint256: 1"
}
```

And if you click on *products*, you should see the product details that you have entered with product id 0.

```
{
        "0": "uint256: id 0",
        "1": "address: seller 0xca35b7d915458ef540ade6068dfe2f44e8fa733c",
        "2": "address: buyer 0x0000000000000000000000000000000000000000",
        "3": "string: name watch",
        "4": "string: description sports watch",
        "5": "uint256: price 0"
}
```

Next, post more products for sale by calling *sellProduct* multiple times and see what happens. *getNumberOfProducts* will increment as you post more products for sale. *products* mapping will also hold the newly added product(s).

Now if you try to call *buyProduct* with id 0 from the same account, i.e. seller tries to buy it's own product, and you click on the 'Details' button in the console you will see the error status: "Transaction mined but execution failed". And that is because buyer has to be different account from seller. The transaction has reverted to its initial state because the *require()* statement executed and we did not meet it's requirement. Note that we have no information inside this error message that indicates that seller should not be equal to buyer. So the specific error is not communicated to us.

To use a different account to buy, switch accounts by using the 'Account' dropdown list (fig. 5.2).

Figure 5.2

Change to another account and now call *buyProduct* with product id 0. If you do not specify 'Value', you will find that your execution once again fails with the same error message. This error message is thrown when a *require* statement in the smart contract evaluates to false. Again, note that the error message is quite generic and doesn't pinpoint exactly why it failed.

But you will realize that it fails this time because our 'Value' doesn't match the product price as enforced by our require statement(s).

```
require(msg.sender != product.seller);
require(msg.value == product.price);
```

Try calling again *buyProduct* with 20 wei as value and the execution should be successful. So we can send ether along to payable functions by specifying the 'Value' property.

Note that if you want to retest a contract on a new instance, make sure that you delete the current instance and re-deploy before re-testing.

Using the Remix Debugger

It can be quite challenging to find out why our contract is failing especially when there are no specific error messages. Remix provides a debugger which can help us. When we made the function call, you see two buttons, 'Details' and 'Debug'. When you click on 'Debug', the right hand panel change to the debugger which allows you to step through the execution of our code (fig. 5.3).

Figure 5.3

The slide bar allows us to fast forward or rewind execution of our contract and you can see when code execution stops. Alternatively, you can drag the slider to the extreme left, then click 'step into' for line by line execution.

Summary

In this chapter, we wrote a real life use case eBay clone smart contract. We were introduced to more Solidity variable types, data structures e.g. mappings, and implemented more complex smart contract functions. In the next chapter, we will begin developing our React user front end for our smart contract.

The full smart contract code for this chapter can be found at https://github.com/greglim81/solidity-chapter5

CHAPTER 6: REACT FRONTEND FOR EBAY SMART CONTRACT

In this chapter, we will be creating our smart contract user front end using React. We will then be really creating a blockchain application that users are comfortable interacting with via their browsers. You can't imagine them using Remix to interact with our contract right? Now why do we use React to develop our frontend and what is React?

You might have heard or read else where that you can use plain vanilla HTML/JavaScript or even jQuery to implement user front ends for your smart contract. Now the problem with using vanilla HTML with JavaScript is that it has its limits especially when you are building more complex UI with lots of logic implemented via JavaScript. You will realize that you have to inevitably write spaghetti code to traverse, add, remove and update elements in your DOM. Now only so, if you decide to change the look of your UI or introduce new features, much of your DOM traversal logic breaks, thus making maintenance of the frontend very difficult.

Fortunately, in recent years, JavaScript frameworks like Angular, React or Vue have been released where you don't write code to manually navigate the DOM. Rather you declare what you want rendered and the framework will manage the DOM for you. This provides a safe and efficient way of manipulating HTML content. And besides, knowing a latest framework like Angular, React or Vue certainly looks good on your resume! I have written books on Angular and React before and do reach out to me on how you can obtain a free copy of it!

In this book, I will be using React to create the user front end. Now, if you are already familiar with React, it would be a breeze. But if this is your first time being exposed to React or you are unfamiliar with it, don't worry. You can contact me at support@i-ducate.com for a free copy of my React book (exclusively for buyers of my Solidity book only!). In this chapter, we will go through the basics of React; what's necessary to implement a simple, yet elegant and intereactive front end for our blockchain eBay clone app. So let's get on with it!

Creating our React Project with Create React App

As sited in the official Reactjs documentation (https://reactjs.org/docs/add-react-to-a-new-app.html):

"Create React App is the best way to start building a new React single page application. It sets up your development environment so that you can use the latest JavaScript features, provides a nice developer experience, and optimizes your app for production. You'll need to have Node >= 6 on your machine.

Create React App doesn't handle backend logic or databases; it just creates a frontend build pipeline, so you can use it with any backend you want. It uses build tools like Babel and webpack under the hood, but works with zero configuration."

So go ahead and install Create React App by running the following commands in Terminal:

```
npm install -g create-react-app
create-react-app ebayclonereact

cd ebayclonereact
npm start
```

You should see the following opened in your browser (fig. 6.1):

To get started, edit `src/App.js` and save to reload.

Figure 6.1

As the message in the browser suggests, you can go ahead and edit App.js in your React project App.js is where we will work most. So open the React project folder in your code editor, (I recommend VSCode) and try changing the welcome message in App.js to something else. What happens? You should see the changed message when your browser reloads automatically.

Before we go on to implement our frontend React code, we will first install the web3 library.

Installing web3

To install the web3 library, open a second Terminal window, go to the React project directory and run:

```
npm install --save web3@1.0.0-beta.34
```

At time of writing, the latest stable version is 1.0.0-beta.34.

web3 Setup

In this section, we will attempt to setup web3 in our React project. Fill in the following codes in bold in App.js of your React project.

App.js

```
import React, { Component } from 'react';
import Web3 from 'web3';

class App extends Component {

  async getAccount(){
    const web3 = new Web3(window.web3.currentProvider);
    const accounts = await web3.eth.getAccounts();
    console.log(accounts[0]);
  }

  render() {
    this.getAccount();
    return (
      <div className="App">
      </div>
    );
  }
}

export default App;
```

Code Explanation

For remove unnecessary cluttering of code, I have removed the default markup in the *render()* method of App to be simply:

```
    return (
      <div className="App">
      </div>
    );
```

* In a React component, implementing the *render()* method is required. When called, it should return a single React element and renders it onto the browser. This element can be either a representation of a native DOM component, such as *<div />*, or another composite component that you've defined yourself. For example, the default App component returns a single *<div />*.

```
import Web3 from 'web3';
```

Just as what we have done with our previous testing and deploy scripts, to begin using web3, we have to import the *Web3* constructor.

```
async getAccount(){
  const web3 = new Web3(window.web3.currentProvider);
  const accounts = await web3.eth.getAccounts();
  console.log(accounts[0]);
}
```

We then create a method called *getAccount()* to house our web3 instantiation code. We have to mark *getAccounts* as *async* because we are using the *await* statement later for an asynchronous method call. Remember that web3 method calls are asynchronous.

For our current app, we assume that the user is running MetaMask. Now when MetaMask runs in a browser, it automatically injects the web3 library into any active page and we provide this web3 library to our constructor with the code `window.web3.currentProvider`. We then proceed to get the first account and log it in the console.

```
render() {
  this.getAccount();
  ...
```

We then call *getAccount()* in *render()*. Now when you save and run this app in the browser, you will see your account address printed in the console.

```
                                            react-dom.development.js:16634
Download the React DevTools for a better development
experience: https://fb.me/react-devtools
0x38B254e5a18C1543c9e0A6C3bC1DB9a14fbe88B0              App.js:9
```

Congratulations! We have successfully setup web3 in our React project.

Deploying the eBayClone Contract

Before we continue with our eBayClone React frontend, we will first need to deploy our eBayClone smart contract on the Rinkeby network. We will have to feed the eBayClone smart contract ABI (the interface between the blockchain world and JavaScript world) into our web3 instance. We will also have to tell web3 the address of the deployed contract. With that, web3 can then communicate with our deployed contract on Rinkeby and call different methods on it.

To deploy our contract, we can follow the same procedures as what we have done when we deployed Greetings.sol. That is, we will need our compile.js and deploy.js file. We won't have to code them from scratch. Rather, copy the *contract* folder containing compile.js, deploy.js for Greetings.sol and other files for e.g. node_modules and then just change the file name in compile.js as shown below:

compile.js

```
const path = require('path');
const fs = require('fs');
const solc = require('solc');

const eBayClonePath = path.resolve(__dirname,'contracts','EBayClone.sol');

const source = fs.readFileSync(eBayClonePath, 'utf8');

module.exports = solc.compile(source, 1).contracts[':EBayClone'];
```

The code for deploy.js would be the same except that in *deploy* function call, we remove the arguments property since our EBayClone smart contract doesn't take in any arguments in its constructor.

deploy.js

```
...
    const result = await new web3.eth.Contract(JSON.parse(interface))
      .deploy({data:'0x'+ bytecode, arguments:['Hello World']})
      .send({from: accounts[0], gas:'5000000'});
...
```

Also, because we need the ABI code and also the address where the contract is deployed, we add the following two console log statements to the end of deploy.js:

```
...
const deploy = async () => {
    accounts = await web3.eth.getAccounts();

    console.log('attempting to deploy from account',accounts[0]);

    const result = await new web3.eth.Contract(JSON.parse(interface))
      .deploy({data:'0x'+ bytecode})
      .send({from: accounts[0], gas:'1000000'});

    console.log(interface);
    console.log('Contract deployed to', result.options.address);
};

deploy();
```

To begin deploying EBayClone.sol, in Terminal in the *contract* directory, run

```
node deploy.js
```

Once again, you can monitor the interacts between your deployed contract in etherscan.io.

Local Contract Instances

Now back in our React app folder, in App.js, add the following lines of code as shown in bold:

```
import React, { Component } from 'react';
import Web3 from 'web3';

class App extends Component {

  web3;
  eBayClone;

  constructor(props, context) {
    super(props, context);
    this.web3 = new Web3(window.web3.currentProvider);

    const address = '...'; // copy from console log of 'node deploy.js'
    const abi = ...; // copy from console log of 'node deploy.js'
    this.eBayClone = new this.web3.eth.Contract(abi, address);
  }

  render() {
    return (
      <div className="App">
      </div>
    );
  }
}

export default App;
```

Code Explanation

```
  constructor(props, context) {
    super(props, context);
    this.web3 = new Web3(window.web3.currentProvider);

    const address = '0x11C1...'; // copy from console
    // copy from console
    const abi = [{"constant":true,"inputs":[],"name":...];
```

```
        this.eBayClone = new this.web3.eth.Contract(abi, address);
    }
```

Now instead of having *getAccount()*, we created a constructor for App.js and moved the web3 instance with MetaMask provider into it.

*Note how *props* is passed to the base constructor with *super(props)*. We should always call the base constructor with *props*. *props* in turn are sent to the superclass by invoking *super()*. The superclass is *React.Component*. Invoking *super* initializes the component instance and *React.Component* decorates that instance with functionality that includes state management which we will cover later

Next, we copy the address and ABI of the deployed eBayClone smart contract from the console and use it as arguments in the *Contract* constructor to create a local contract instance that survives in our browser. The local contract instance serves as a connection to our deployed contract on the blockchain which we use to connect our React project.

Rendering Contract Data

We will first show the header bar of our site with the current user address and how much balance she has in her Ethereum account.

eBay Clone   Signed in as: 0x06FdF0332B250617bF7C9F44eEf24593A8353060   Balance: 0.337664095999999989

To do so, we first declare a state object below our constructor:

```
...
  constructor(props, context) {
      ...
  }
  state = {
    user:'',
    balance: ''
  };
...
```

*The concept of 'state' in React components is that state manages data that will change within a component. Whenever state changes, the UI is rerendered to reflect those changes. We often refer to this as the component or local state. To add local state to our component, we declare our initial state as a single object below our constructor that can contain one or more attributes. Our current state is an object containing a two attributes *user* and *balance*.

We then create a method *refreshContractDetails* marked as *async*:

```
async refreshContractDetails(){
  const accounts = await this.web3.eth.getAccounts();
  const user = accounts[0];
  const balance = this.web3.utils.fromWei(await
this.web3.eth.getBalance(user),'ether');
  this.setState({
    user: user,
    balance: balance
  });
}
```

Inside *refreshContractDetails*, we get the user account with *await this.web3.eth.getAccounts()*, and the balance using *await this.web3.eth.getBalance(user)*. Now this returns us the balance in terms of wei, which will be a very huge number. By convention and eligibility, applications show prices and amounts in ethers.

web3.js provides the *fromWei()* method to convert wei to any other unit and the *toWei()* method to convert any other unit into wei. So we convert from wei to ether using *this.web3.utils.fromWei* and specifying 'ether' as the 2nd argument. The 2nd argument can be either of the below:
-   kwei/ada
-   mwei/babbage
-   gwei/shannon
-   szabo
-   finney
-   ether
-   kether/grand/einstein
-   mether
-   gether
-   tether

Now how do we call *refreshContractDetails*? We call *refreshContractDetails* in the React lifecycle method *componentDidMount*. *componentDidMount()* is called after the first render of the component. This is where data requests and DOM or state updates should occur. In terms of lifecycle, *componentDidMount()* is called after the constructor.

```
componentDidMount(){
  this.refreshContractDetails();
}
```

And to render *user* and *balance*, we add the following into *render()*:

```
render() {
  return (
    <div className="App">
      User: {this.state.user}
      <br/>
      Balance: {this.state.balance}
    </div>
  );
}
```

When you run your app now, you should get something like the below rendered in your browser (fig. 6.2).

←   C ⟳   ⓘ localhost:3000

User: 0x38B254e5a18C1543c9e0A6C3bC1DB9a14fbe88B0
Balance: 1.166752871000000011

Figure 6.2

Although it doesn't look too professional currently (we will address that shortly in the next section), it shows that we have successfully connected our Ethereum account to our React project.

At the moment, your App.js should look something like:

```
import React, { Component } from 'react';
import Web3 from 'web3';

class App extends Component {

  web3;
  eBayClone;

  constructor(props, context) {
    super(props, context);
    this.web3 = new Web3(window.web3.currentProvider);

    const address = '0x11C1B3F4A231652b57…';
    const abi = [{"constant":true,"inputs":[],"name":…];
    this.eBayClone = new this.web3.eth.Contract(abi, address);
  }
  state = {
    user:'',
    balance: ''
  };
```

71

```
  componentDidMount(){
    this.refreshContractDetails();
  }

  async refreshContractDetails(){
    const accounts = await this.web3.eth.getAccounts();
    const user = accounts[0];
    const balance = this.web3.utils.fromWei(await
this.web3.eth.getBalance(user),'ether');
    this.setState({
      user: user,
      balance: balance
    });
  }

  render() {
    return (
      <div className="App">
        User: {this.state.user}
        <br/>
        Balance: {this.state.balance}
      </div>
    );
  }
}

export default App;
```

Using React Bootstrap to Beautify Our UI

To make our UI more professional, we will install react bootstrap (https://react-bootstrap.github.io/), a popular front end framework. To install react bootstrap, go to your React project and run the following in the Terminal (refer to https://react-bootstrap.github.io/getting-started/introduction/):

```
npm install --save react react-dom
npm install --save react-bootstrap
```

Next, copy and include the bootstrap stylesheet link from (https://react-bootstrap.github.io/getting-started/introduction/) into index.html in your React project *public* folder. It should look something like:

<link rel="stylesheet" href="https://maxcdn.bootstrapcdn.com/bootstrap/3.3.7/css/bootstrap.min.css" integrity="sha384-BVYiiSIFeK1dGmJRAkycuHAHRg32OmUcww7on3RYdg4Va+PmSTsz/K68vbdEjh4u" crossorigin="anonymous">

React bootstrap provides several components that we can use to build our front end. To build our navigation bar header, we will use the *navbar* 'Text and Non-nav links' component (https://react-bootstrap.github.io/components/navbar/) with the following markup:

```
<Navbar>
  <Navbar.Header>
    <Navbar.Brand>
      <a href="#home">Brand</a>
    </Navbar.Brand>
    <Navbar.Toggle />
  </Navbar.Header>
  <Navbar.Collapse>
    <Navbar.Text>
      Signed in as: <Navbar.Link href="#">Mark Otto</Navbar.Link>
    </Navbar.Text>
    <Navbar.Text pullRight>Have a great day!</Navbar.Text>
  </Navbar.Collapse>
</Navbar>;
```

Copy the markup in to the *render()* method and make the changes as shown in **bold** below:

```
  render() {
    return (
      <div className="App">
        <Navbar>
          <Navbar.Header>
            <Navbar.Brand>
              <a href="#home">eBay Clone</a>
            </Navbar.Brand>
            <Navbar.Toggle />
          </Navbar.Header>
          <Navbar.Collapse>
            <Navbar.Text>
              Signed in as: <Navbar.Link href="#">{this.state.user}</Navbar.Link>
            </Navbar.Text>
            <Navbar.Text pullRight>Balance: {this.state.balance}</Navbar.Text>
          </Navbar.Collapse>
        </Navbar>;
      </div>
    );
  }
```

You will have to include the import statement for *Navbar* as shown below:

```
import React, { Component } from 'react';
import Web3 from 'web3';
import { Navbar } from 'react-bootstrap';
...
```

Now when you run your React app, it should like something like:

Now that we have installed react bootstrap into our project and rendered our header bar successfully, let's go on to include a button where a user can click to popup the Sell Product form.

Sell Product Modal Form

Because we want a popup form for our sell product form, (rather than navigating to another webpage to show the form), we will use the Modal component basic example (https://react-bootstrap.github.io/components/modal/) with the following code additions in the markup:

```
render() {
  return (
    <div className="App">
      <Navbar>
        <Navbar.Header>
          <Navbar.Brand>
            <a href="#home">eBay Clone</a>
          </Navbar.Brand>
          <Navbar.Toggle />
        </Navbar.Header>
        <Navbar.Collapse>
          <Navbar.Text>
            Signed in as: <Navbar.Link
href="#">{this.state.user}</Navbar.Link>
          </Navbar.Text>
          <Navbar.Text>Balance: {this.state.balance}</Navbar.Text>
          <Navbar.Text pullRight>
            <Button onClick={this.handleShow}>Sell an article</Button>
          </Navbar.Text>
        </Navbar.Collapse>
      </Navbar>;
      <Modal show={this.state.show} onHide={this.handleClose}>
        <Modal.Header closeButton>
          <Modal.Title>Sell a Product </Modal.Title>
        </Modal.Header>
        <Modal.Body>
```

74

```
      </Modal.Body>
      <Modal.Footer>
        <Button onClick={this.handleClose}>Close</Button>
        <Button onClick={this.handleSell}>Sell</Button>
      </Modal.Footer>
    </Modal>
  </div>
);
}
```

Code Explanation

```
      <Navbar.Collapse>
        <Navbar.Text>
          Signed in as: <Navbar.Link href="#">{this.state.user}</Navbar.Link>
        </Navbar.Text>
        <Navbar.Text>Balance: {this.state.balance}</Navbar.Text>
        <Navbar.Text pullRight>
          <Button onClick={this.handleShow}>Sell a Product</Button>
        </Navbar.Text>
      </Navbar.Collapse>
```

First, we add a new "Sell a Product" button into our *Navbar*. We set the button to the right of the navbar with the *pullright* directive.

The event handler for our Button is the *handleShow* method. We will explain the implementation of the *handleShow* method shortly.

```
      <Modal show={this.state.show} onHide={this.handleClose}>
        <Modal.Header closeButton>
          <Modal.Title>Sell a Product </Modal.Title>
        </Modal.Header>
        <Modal.Body>
        </Modal.Body>
        <Modal.Footer>
          <Button onClick={this.handleClose}>Close</Button>
          <Button onClick={this.handleSell}>Sell</Button>
        </Modal.Footer>
      </Modal>
```

Next, below the Navbar component, we have the Modal component. The default markup for the Modal component has been deliberately removed of many unnecessary sub components since we don't want unnecessary code clutter.

handleShow

The *show* property of Modal is set to *this.state.show*. This means that we hide this Modal whenever *state.show* is false and show the form when *state.show* is true. Thus in *handleShow*, we need to switch *state.show* to *true* in state with the following code:

```
handleShow() {
  this.setState({
    show: true
  });
}
```

We obviously need to add *show* to our state just below our constructor with the following code:

```
state = {
  user:'',
  balance: '',
  show: false
};
```

Also make sure that you have imported the Modal and Button component from react bootstrap with the following import statement:

```
import { Navbar, Modal, Button } from 'react-bootstrap';
```

handleClose

Next, note that you in Modal footer, we show the Close button.

```
<Modal.Footer>
  <Button onClick={this.handleClose}>Close</Button>
</Modal.Footer>
```

The *Close* button should trigger the *onClick* event which calls *handleClose* when clicked. The *onHide* event (called when you click on the 'X' on the Modal popup) should similarly call *handleClose*.

```
<Modal show={this.state.show} onHide={this.handleClose}>
```

handleClose is similarly to *handleShow* except that it sets *show* in state to false.

```
handleClose() {
  this.setState({
    show: false
  });
}
```

Finally, in the constructor, we bind the two methods *handleShow* and *handleClose* by adding the below codes:

```
constructor(props, context) {
  super(props, context);
  this.web3 = new Web3(window.web3.currentProvider);

  const address = '0x11C1B3F4A231652b572454cC59c8B4Ee76dE588b';
  const abi = …
  this.eBayClone = new this.web3.eth.Contract(abi, address);

  this.handleShow = this.handleShow.bind(this);
  this.handleClose = this.handleClose.bind(this);
}
state = {
  user:'',
  balance: '',
  show: false
};
```

The two bind statements above binds the *handleShow* and *handleClose* function to our component.

Running our App

Now when you run your app and click on 'Sell a Product', you will be shown the Modal.

And when you click on either 'X' or 'Close', the Modal hides. Next, we will add form elements such as field inputs for product name, description and price into the Modal form.

Adding the form

Add the following inside the *Modal.Body* element (the form markup is taken from https://react-bootstrap.github.io/components/forms/):

```
<Modal.Body>
  <form>
    <FormGroup
      controlId="formBasicText"
```

```
                >
                  <ControlLabel>Product name</ControlLabel>
                  <FormControl
                    type="text"
                    value={this.state.productName}
                    placeholder="Enter the name of your product"
                    onChange={this.handleProductNameChange}
                  />
                  <ControlLabel>Price in ETH</ControlLabel>
                  <FormControl
                    type="number"
                    value={this.state.productPrice}
                    placeholder="1"
                    onChange={this.handleProductPriceChange}
                  />
                  <ControlLabel>Description</ControlLabel>
                  <FormControl
                    type="text"
                    value={this.state.productDescription}
                    placeholder="Describe your article"
                    onChange={this.handleProductDescChange}
                  />
                </FormGroup>
              </form>
            </Modal.Body>
```

This will show the product name, price and description labels and input fields in the form. Remember to import *FormGroup*, *ControlLabel* and *FormControl* from react bootstrap with the below import statement:

```
import { Navbar, Modal, Button, FormGroup, ControlLabel, FormControl }
from 'react-bootstrap';
```

Now when you run your app and open your 'Sell Product' form, it should look like (fig. 6.3):

Figure 6.3

Notice in our FormControls that we have referred to *this.state.productName*, *productPrice* and *productDescription*. We thus need to add them to our initial state just after the constructor as shown in **bold**:

```
constructor(props, context) {
  super(props, context);
  ...

  this.handleShow = this.handleShow.bind(this);
  this.handleClose = this.handleClose.bind(this);
}
state = {
  user:'',
  balance: '',
  show: false,
  productName:'',
  productDescription:'',
  productPrice:''
};
```

Also notice the *onChange* event in FormControls is linked to *handleProductName*, *handleProductPrice* and *handleProductDescription*. Implement them as follows:

```
handleProductNameChange(e) {
  this.setState({ productName: e.target.value });
}
handleProductDescChange(e) {
```

```
      this.setState({ productDescription: e.target.value });
  }
  handleProductPriceChange(e) {
      this.setState({ productPrice: e.target.value });
  }
```

What happens in our FormControl is that we displayed the value as stored in our *state* object. But when user keys something into the input box, the *onChange* event is called and we update the state which in turn updates the value displayed in the input box. Such a pattern is common in React forms.

```
  handleShow() {
    this.setState({
      show: true,
      productName: '',
      productPrice: '',
      productDescription: ''
    });
  }
```

Now for *handleShow()*, we set product name, price and description to blank whenever we show the form. This is to ensure that we have a fresh new form with no old values populated.

```
    constructor(props, context) {
      super(props, context);
      this.web3 = new Web3(window.web3.currentProvider);

      const address = '0x11C1B3F4A231652b572454cC59c8B4Ee76dE588b';
      const abi = …
      this.eBayClone = new this.web3.eth.Contract(abi, address);

      this.handleShow = this.handleShow.bind(this);
      this.handleClose = this.handleClose.bind(this);
      this.handleProductDescChange = this.handleProductDescChange.bind(this);
      this.handleProductNameChange = this.handleProductNameChange.bind(this);
      this.handleProductPriceChange = this.handleProductPriceChange.bind(this);
    }
```

Just as we have binded *handleShow* and *handleClose* to our component in the constructor, we also bind *handleProductDescChange*, *handleProductNameChange* and *handleProductPriceChange*.

handleSell

Next, we need to add a 'Sell' button which takes in the inputs the user has entered and proceed to call *sellProduct* function in our deployed smart contract (fig. 6.4).

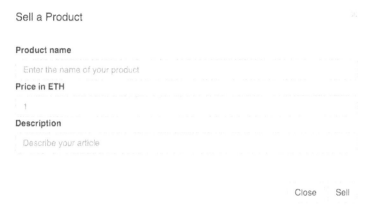

Figure 6.4

```
<Modal.Footer>
  <Button onClick={this.handleClose}>Close</Button>
  <Button onClick={this.handleSell}>Sell</Button>
</Modal.Footer>
```

In the above code, we add a 'Sell' button in the Modal footer with the *handleSell* function.

```
handleSell = async (event) => {
  event.preventDefault();
  this.setState({message: "waiting on sell transaction success..."});
  this.handleClose();
  await this.eBayClone.methods.sellProduct(this.state.productName,
    this.state.productDescription,
    this.web3.utils.toWei(this.state.productPrice,'ether'))
    .send({
        from:this.state.user,
        gas:500000
    });

  await this.refreshContractDetails();
  this.setState({message: "Sell transaction entered"});
}
```

Notice that before we call *sellProduct* on our deployed contract, we *setState* message to "waiting on sell transaction success...". This is because we want to tell the user about the state of our app while our transaction is going on. And after the transaction completes, we call *setState* message again this time setting the message to "`Sell transaction entered`".

Thus, we need to add *message* to our component state:

```
state = {
  user:'',
  balance: '',
  show: false,
  productName:'',
  productDescription:'',
  productPrice:'',
  message:''
};
```

We also render the message on the top of our screen:

```
render() {
  return (
    <div className="App">
      <h1>{this.state.message}</h1>
      <Navbar>
        <Navbar.Header>
```

Now when you run your app, click 'Sell a Product', enter your product details and click 'Sell', the 'Sell a Product' popup should close and a MetaMask notification form to confirm your transaction should appear (fig. 6.5):

Figure 6.5

When you click on 'Submit', the transaction will be sent to the contract. The message 'waiting on sell transaction success…' will be displayed on the top.

waiting on sell transaction success…

After around 20-30 seconds, the message should change to 'Sell transaction entered'.

Sell transaction entered

Congratulations! We have just called our first function on our deployed contract through the React user front end. In the next section, we will see how to display the list of products we have posted for sale.

Displaying List of Products

To display the list of products, we would need to add a **products** array to store the product results returned from the blockchain:

```
state = {
  user:'',
  balance: '',
  show: false,
  productName:'',
  productDescription:'',
  productPrice:'',
  message:'',
  products:[]
};
```

Retrieving Products

We then populate the products array in *refreshContractDetails* with the below codes in **bold**:

```
async refreshContractDetails(){
  const accounts = await this.web3.eth.getAccounts();
  const user = accounts[0];
  const balance = this.web3.utils.fromWei(await
this.web3.eth.getBalance(user),'ether');

  const productsCount = await
this.eBayClone.methods.getNumberOfProducts().call();
  const products = await Promise.all(
    Array(parseInt(productsCount))
      .fill()
      .map((element,index) => {
        return this.eBayClone.methods.products(index).call();
      })
  );

  this.setState({
    user: user,
    balance: balance,
    products:products
  });
}
```

We first get the number of products with `await`

84

```
this.eBayClone.methods.getNumberOfProducts().call()
```

We then use *map* to call and return each *product* from *products* array in our smart contract by providing it with the below function as argument to map:

```
.map((element,index) => {
  return this.eBayClone.methods.products(index).call();
})
```

map loops through each element and makes the function call to each individual *product* in *products* in the smart contract. These then fills our React component *products* array with `Array(parseInt(productsCount)).fill()`.

We then wrap all these individual function calls to our smart contract with *Promise.all* to return us a single Promise that resolves when all of the promises in it have resolved. That is, we issue all of the request to get each product in one go and then wait for them all to be resolved by using *Promise.All.*

The end result would be that *products* array will contain all our requested products.

Rendering Products

To render each product, we will import the *ListGroup* and *ListGroupItem* components from react bootstrap.

```
import { Navbar, Modal, Button, FormGroup, ControlLabel, FormControl,
ListGroup, ListGroupItem } from 'react-bootstrap';
```

We then render them with the *renderProducts()* function:

```
renderProducts(){
  return this.state.products.map((product, index) =>{
    var price = this.web3.utils.fromWei(product.price,'ether');
    return(
        <ListGroup>
          <ListGroupItem header={product.name}>Description
{product.description}</ListGroupItem>
          <ListGroupItem>Price (ETH) {price}</ListGroupItem>
          <ListGroupItem>Sold by {product.seller}</ListGroupItem>
          <ListGroupItem>Bought by {product.buyer}</ListGroupItem>
        </ListGroup>
    );
  });
}
```

In *renderProducts()*, we similarly use *map* to return a *ListGroup* element for each product. We pass in a function into *map* which loops through each *product*, calls the function that returns a *ListGroup* element for each product, and are returned a new array of products which can then be rendered in *render()*.

Thus in *render()*, add the call to *renderProducts()*:

```
<Modal.Footer>
  <Button onClick={this.handleClose}>Close</Button>
  <Button onClick={this.handleSell}>Sell</Button>
</Modal.Footer>
</Modal>
{this.renderProducts()}
</div>
);
```

When you run your app now, you should see your products rendered (fig. 6.6):

eBay Clone   Signed in as: 0x38B254e5a18C1543c9e0A6C3bC1DB9a14fbe88B0   Balance: 1.166478263000000011   Sell a Product

Product1
Description Product1Desc

Price (ETH) 0.1

Sold by 0x38B254e5a18C1543c9e0A6C3bC1DB9a14fbe88B0

Bought by 0x0000000000000000000000000000000000000000

Product2
Description Product2desc

Price (ETH) 0.01

Sold by 0x38B254e5a18C1543c9e0A6C3bC1DB9a14fbe88B0

Bought by 0x0000000000000000000000000000000000000000

Figure 6.6

Adding a Buy Button

In this section, we will add a buy button to each product listing. Before we render the buy button, we implement a function called *handleBuy* which the buy button will call. Implement *handleBuy* as shown below:

handleBuy

```
handleBuy = (_productId,_productPrice,_productSeller) => async(event)=> {
```

86

```
    event.preventDefault();
    if( productSeller == this.state.user){
      this.setState({message: "You cannot buy your own product."});
      return;
    }

    this.setState({message: "waiting on buy transaction..."});
    await this.eBayClone.methods. buyProduct ( productId).send({
      from:this.state.user,
      value: this.web3.utils.toWei( productPrice,'ether'),
      gas:500000
    });

    this.setState({message: "Buy transaction entered"});
    await this.refreshContractDetails();
};
```

Code Explanation

```
handleBuy = ( productId, productPrice, productSeller) => async(event)=> {
    event.preventDefault();
```

handleBuy takes in the product id, price and seller as argument.

```
    if( productSeller == this.state.user){
      this.setState({message: "You cannot buy your own product."});
      return;
    }
```

It then checks if the product seller is equal to the current user of the app. And if so, we show the message than a user cannot buy her own product and then exit the function.

```
    this.setState({message: "waiting on buy transaction..."});
    await this.eBayClone.methods.buyProduct( productId).send({
      from:this.state.user,
      value: this.web3.utils.toWei( productPrice,'ether'),
      gas:500000
    });
```

If the user is not the product seller, we proceed and set the message to "waiting on buy transaction…". We then proceed to call *buyProduct* in our deployed contract with product id as argument, and we set value to be the product price.

```
    this.setState({message: "Buy transaction entered"});
    await this.refreshContractDetails();
```

When the transaction completes successfully, we set the message to "Buy transaction entered" and refresh contract details.

Rendering the Buy Button

To render the *buy* button in each product listing, we add the codes in **bold** to *renderProducts()*:

```
renderProducts(){
  return this.state.products.map((product, index) =>{
    var price = this.web3.utils.fromWei(product.price,'ether');
    return(
        <ListGroup>
          <ListGroupItem header={product.name}>Description
{product.description}</ListGroupItem>
          <ListGroupItem>Price (ETH) {price}</ListGroupItem>
          <ListGroupItem>Sold by {product.seller}</ListGroupItem>
          <ListGroupItem>Bought by {product.buyer}</ListGroupItem>
          <ListGroupItem>
            <Button bsStyle="primary"
                  onClick={this.handleBuy(product.id,price,product.seller)}>
              Buy
            </Button>
          </ListGroupItem>
        </ListGroup>
    );
  });
}
```

We add a new *ListGroupItem* which contains a *Button* with *onClick* calling *handleBuy* with id, price and seller as arguments.

When you run your app now, you should see the buy button in each product listing (fig. 6.7).

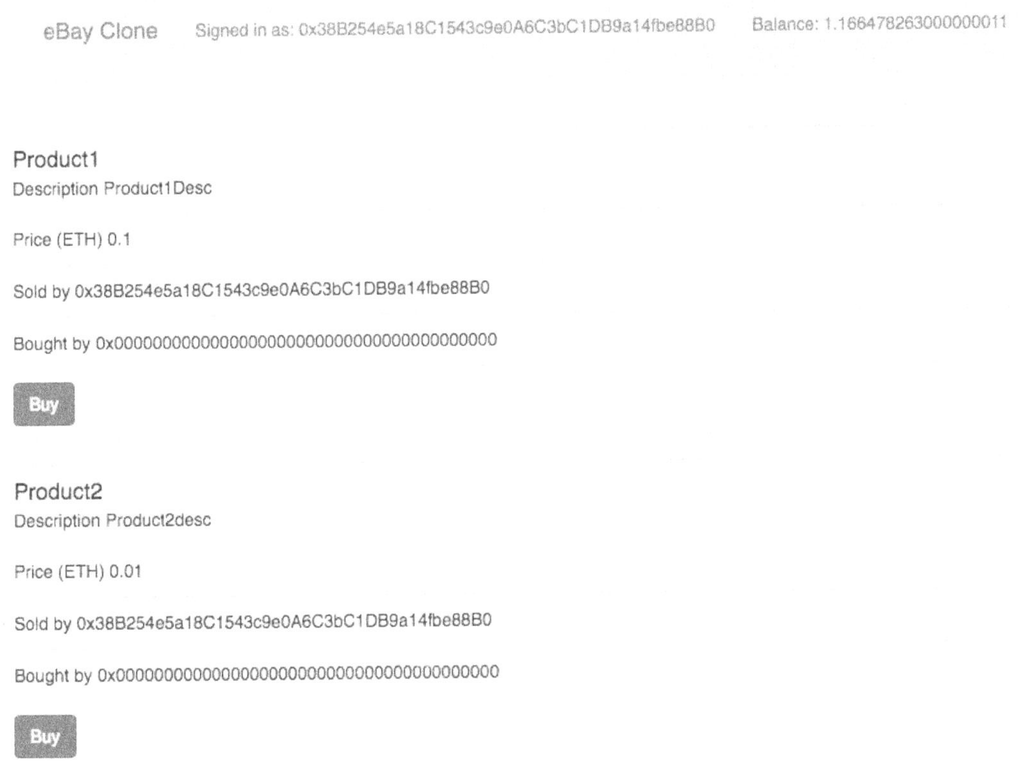

eBay Clone   Signed in as: 0x38B254e5a18C1543c9e0A6C3bC1DB9a14fbe88B0   Balance: 1.166478263000000011

Product1
Description Product1Desc

Price (ETH) 0.1

Sold by 0x38B254e5a18C1543c9e0A6C3bC1DB9a14fbe88B0

Bought by 0x0000000000000000000000000000000000000000

Product2
Description Product2desc

Price (ETH) 0.01

Sold by 0x38B254e5a18C1543c9e0A6C3bC1DB9a14fbe88B0

Bought by 0x0000000000000000000000000000000000000000

Figure 6.7

And assuming you have not changed accounts in MetaMask, if you try to buy any of the product you have posted for sale, you should get the message (fig. 6.8):

You cannot buy your own product.

eBay Clone   Signed in as: 0x38B254e5a18C1543c9e0A6C3bC1DB9a14fbe88B0   Balance: 1.166478263000000011

Figure 6.8

Now so how do we test our app since we cannot sell and buy with the same account?

Back in MetaMask, click on the ⊕ logo and there will be an option where you can 'Create Account' (fig. 6.9).

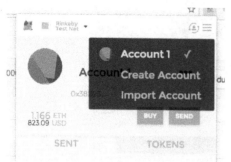

Rinkeby
Test Net
Account 1
Create Account
Import Account
1.166 ETH
823.09 USD
BUY
SEND
SENT
TOKENS
Figure 6.9

In the new account, get some ethers by going to https://faucet.rinkeby.io/ (we have done this previously in chapter four). With this new account, try refreshing the page and click on 'buy' again for one of the posted products. You should again see the MetaMask notification popup appear with the 'amount' being the product price amount. Go ahead and click submit and the 'waiting on buy transaction' message should appear (fig. 6.10).

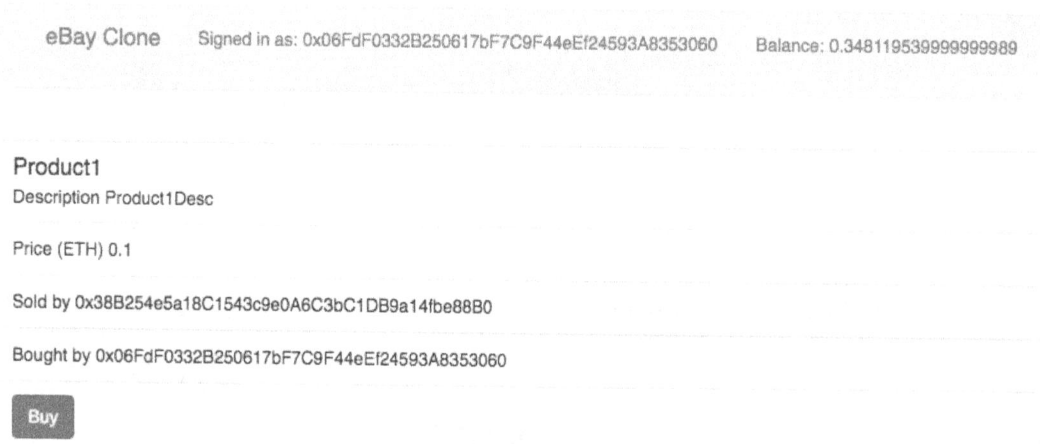

eBay Clone
Signed in as: 0x06FdF0332B250617bF7C9F44eEf24593A8353060
Balance: 0.348119539999999989
Product1
Description Product1Desc
Price (ETH) 0.1
Sold by 0x38B254e5a18C1543c9e0A6C3bC1DB9a14fbe88B0
Bought by 0x06FdF0332B250617bF7C9F44eEf24593A8353060
Buy
Figure 6.10

The transation should complete successfully after 20-30 seconds and the *Bought By* field which initally shows '0x0000000…' will now show the buyer address.

Filtering Bought Items

Currently, we are showing all products, including those that have not been bought and those that have been bought. Ideally, we should filter away products that have been bought, since they can no longer be bought and would add clutter to our site. To show only products that have not been bought, we add the following *if* clause as shown:

```
renderProducts(){
  return this.state.products.map((product, index) =>{
    if( product.buyer == 0x0){
      var price = this.web3.utils.fromWei(product.price,'ether');
      return(
        <ListGroup>
          <ListGroupItem header={product.name}>Description
              {product.description}</ListGroupItem>
          <ListGroupItem>Price (ETH) {price}</ListGroupItem>
          <ListGroupItem>Sold by {product.seller}</ListGroupItem>
          <ListGroupItem>Bought by {product.buyer}</ListGroupItem>
          <ListGroupItem>
            <Button bsStyle="primary"
                onClick={this.handleBuy(product.id,price,product.seller)}>
              Buy
            </Button>
          </ListGroupItem>
        </ListGroup>
      );
    }
  });
```

When you run your app again, it would now show only products that have not been bought.

Summary

We have gone through quite a lot to implement our React front end for our smart contract. Our entire React front end is contained in App.js. A more complex app for example with navigation to other pages would require more complex React code which is beyond the scope of this book. If you are interested, you can get a free copy of my React book by sending me a mail at support@i-ducate.com. For now, I have purposely placed everything in a single App.js for simplicity so that you will not be overwhelmed with React code since this book is primarily about Solidity.

In this chapter, we were introduced to the basics of React and used it create our user front end for our eBay clone smart contract. We learnt how to setup web3 and used it to link our contract and our React code. We used React Bootstrap to create a professional looking user interface and when through React basics like creating, submitting forms and rendering lists of data.

Although we have created an eBay clone, we could extend the same concepts to other kinds of decentralized applications like a Twitter clone, fintech apps etc. With this knowledge, you can move on and build more complicated enterprise level fully functional Ethereum decentralized applications of your own!

Hopefully, you have enjoyed this book and would like to learn more from me. I would love to get your feedback, learning what you liked and didn't for us to improve.

Please feel free to email me at support@i-ducate.com if you encounter any errors with your code or to get updated versions of this book. Visit my GitHub repository at https://github.com/greglim81 if you have not already to have the full source code for this book.

If you didn't like the book, or if you feel that I should have covered certain additional topics, please email us to let us know. This book can only get better thanks to readers like you.

If you like the book, I would appreciate if you could leave us a review too.
Thank you and all the best for your learning journey in Ethereum and Solidity!

In case you missed anything, here is the entire code of App.js. Alternatively, you can go to https://github.com/greglim81/solidity-chapter6 to get it.

App.js (Complete Code)

```
import React, { Component } from 'react';
import Web3 from 'web3';
import { Navbar, Modal, Button, FormGroup, ControlLabel, FormControl, ListGroup,
ListGroupItem } from 'react-bootstrap';

class App extends Component {

  web3;
  eBayClone;

  constructor(props, context) {
    super(props, context);
    this.web3 = new Web3(window.web3.currentProvider);

    const address = '0x11C1B3F4A231652b572454cC59c8B4Ee76dE588b';
    const abi =
       [{"constant":true,"inputs":[],"name":"getNumberOfProducts",…
    this.eBayClone = new this.web3.eth.Contract(abi, address);

    this.handleShow = this.handleShow.bind(this);
    this.handleClose = this.handleClose.bind(this);
    this.handleProductDescChange = this.handleProductDescChange.bind(this);
    this.handleProductNameChange = this.handleProductNameChange.bind(this);
    this.handleProductPriceChange = this.handleProductPriceChange.bind(this);
  }
  state = {
    user:'',
    balance: '',
    show: false,
    productName:'',
    productDescription:'',
```

```
      productPrice:'',
      message:'',
      products:[]
    };

    handleClose() {
      this.setState({
        show: false
      });
    }

    handleShow() {
      this.setState({
        show: true,
        productName: '',
        productPrice: '',
        productDescription: ''
      });
    }

    handleProductNameChange(e) {
      this.setState({ productName: e.target.value });
    }
    handleProductDescChange(e) {
      this.setState({ productDescription: e.target.value });
    }
    handleProductPriceChange(e) {
      this.setState({ productPrice: e.target.value });
    }

    componentDidMount(){
      this.refreshContractDetails();
    }

    async refreshContractDetails(){
      const accounts = await this.web3.eth.getAccounts();
      const user = accounts[0];
      const balance = this.web3.utils.fromWei(await
this.web3.eth.getBalance(user),'ether');

      const productsCount = await
        this.eBayClone.methods.getNumberOfProducts().call();
      const products = await Promise.all(
        Array(parseInt(productsCount))
          .fill()
          .map((element,index) => {
            return this.eBayClone.methods.products(index).call();

          })
      );

      this.setState({
```

```
        user: user,
        balance: balance,
        products:products
    });
}

handleSell = async (event) => {
    event.preventDefault();
    this.setState({message: "waiting on sell transaction success…"});
    this.handleClose();
    await this.eBayClone.methods.sellProduct(
        this.state.productName,
        this.state.productDescription,
        this.web3.utils.toWei(this.state.productPrice,'ether')).send({
        from:this.state.user,
        gas:500000
    });

    await this.refreshContractDetails();
    this.setState({message: "Sell transaction entered"});
}

handleBuy = (_productId,_productPrice,_productSeller) => async(event) => {
    event.preventDefault();
    if(_productSeller == this.state.user){
        this.setState({message: "You cannot buy your own product."});
        return;
    }

    this.setState({message: "waiting on buy transaction..."});
    await this.eBayClone.methods.buyProduct(_productId).send({
        from:this.state.user,
        value: this.web3.utils.toWei(_productPrice,'ether'),
        gas:500000
    });

    this.setState({message: "Buy transaction entered"});
    await this.refreshContractDetails();
};

renderProducts(){
    return this.state.products.map((product, index) =>{
        if( product.buyer == 0x0){ // show only articles that have not been bought
            var price = this.web3.utils.fromWei(product.price,'ether');
            return(
                <ListGroup>
                    <ListGroupItem header={product.name}>Description
                            {product.description}</ListGroupItem>
                    <ListGroupItem>Price (ETH) {price}</ListGroupItem>
                    <ListGroupItem>Sold by {product.seller}</ListGroupItem>
                    <ListGroupItem>Bought by {product.buyer}</ListGroupItem>
                    <ListGroupItem>
```

94

```
              <Button bsStyle="primary"
                  onClick={this.handleBuy(product.id,price,product.seller)}>
                Buy
              </Button>
            </ListGroupItem>
          </ListGroup>
      );
    }
  });
}

render() {
  return (
    <div className="App">
      <h1>{this.state.message}</h1>
      <Navbar>
        <Navbar.Header>
          <Navbar.Brand>
            <a href="#home">eBay Clone</a>
          </Navbar.Brand>
          <Navbar.Toggle />
        </Navbar.Header>
        <Navbar.Collapse>
          <Navbar.Text>
            Signed in as: <Navbar.Link href="#">{this.state.user}</Navbar.Link>
          </Navbar.Text>
          <Navbar.Text>Balance: {this.state.balance}</Navbar.Text>
          <Navbar.Text pullRight>
            <Button onClick={this.handleShow}>Sell a Product</Button>
          </Navbar.Text>
        </Navbar.Collapse>
      </Navbar>;
      <Modal show={this.state.show} onHide={this.handleClose}>
        <Modal.Header closeButton>
          <Modal.Title>Sell a Product</Modal.Title>
        </Modal.Header>
        <Modal.Body>
        <form>
            <FormGroup
              controlId="formBasicText"
            >
              <ControlLabel>Product name</ControlLabel>
              <FormControl
                type="text"
                value={this.state.productName}
                placeholder="Enter the name of your product"
                onChange={this.handleProductNameChange}
              />
              <ControlLabel>Price in ETH</ControlLabel>
              <FormControl
                type="number"
                value={this.state.productPrice}
```

```
                    placeholder="1"
                    onChange={this.handleProductPriceChange}
                  />
                  <ControlLabel>Description</ControlLabel>
                  <FormControl
                    type="text"
                    value={this.state.productDescription}
                    placeholder="Describe your article"
                    onChange={this.handleProductDescChange}
                  />
                </FormGroup>
              </form>
            </Modal.Body>
            <Modal.Footer>
              <Button onClick={this.handleClose}>Close</Button>
              <Button onClick={this.handleSell}>Sell</Button>
            </Modal.Footer>
          </Modal>
          {this.renderProducts()}
        </div>
      );
    }
  }

export default App;
```

About the Author

Greg Lim is a technologist and author of several programming books. Greg has many years in teaching programming in tertiary institutions and he places special emphasis on learning by doing.

Contact Greg at support@i-ducate.com.

9 789811 477980